Mystery of the Wax Museum

Wisconsin/Warner Bros. Screenplay Series

Mystery of
the Wax Museum

Edited with an introduction by

Richard Koszarski

Published for the Wisconsin Center for Film and Theater Research by
The University of Wisconsin Press

Published 1979

The University of Wisconsin Press
114 North Murray Street
Madison, Wisconsin 53715

The University of Wisconsin Press, Ltd.
1 Gower Street
London WC1E 6HA, England

First printing

Printed in the United States of America

For LC CIP information see the colophon

ISBN 0-299-07670-9 cloth; 0-299-07674-1 paper

Cover photograph: The Museum of Modern Art/Film Stills Archive, New York

Contents

Foreword

In donating the Warner Film Library to the Wisconsin Center for Film and Theater Research in 1969, along with the RKO and Monogram film libraries and UA corporate records, United Artists created a truly great resource for the study of American film. Acquired by United Artists in 1957, during a period when the major studios sold off their films for use on television, the Warner library is by far the richest portion of the gift, containing eight hundred sound features, fifteen hundred short subjects, nineteen thousand still negatives, legal files, and press books, in addition to screenplays for the bulk of the Warner Brothers product from 1930 to 1950. For the purposes of this project, the company has granted the Center whatever publication rights it holds to the Warner films. In so doing, UA has provided the Center another opportunity to advance the cause of film scholarship.

Our goal in publishing these Warner Brothers screenplays is to explicate the art of screenwriting during the thirties and forties, the so-called Golden Age of Hollywood. In preparing a critical introduction and annotating the screenplay, the editor of each volume is asked to cover such topics as the development of the screenplay from its source to the final shooting script, differences between the final shooting script and the release print, production information, exploitation and critical reception of the film, its historical importance, its directorial style, and its position within the genre. He is also encouraged to go beyond these guidelines to incorporate supplemental information concerning the studio system of motion picture production.

We could set such an ambitious goal because of the richness of the script files in the Warner Film Library. For many film titles, the files might contain the property (novel, play, short story, or original story idea), research materials, variant drafts of scripts (from story outline to treatment to shooting script), post-production items such as press books and dialogue continuities, and legal records (details of the acquisition of the property, copyright registration, and contracts with actors and directors). Editors of the Wisconsin/Warner Bros. Screenplay Series receive copies of all the materials, along with prints of the films (the most authoritative ones available for reference purposes), to use in preparing the introductions and annotating the final shooting scripts.

In the process of preparing the screenplays for publication, typographical errors were corrected, punctuation and capitalization were modernized, and the format was redesigned to facilitate readability. The illustrations for *Mystery of the Wax Museum* are frame enlargements taken from a 16-mm print of the film provided by United Artists.

In theory, the Center should have received the extant scripts of all pre-1951 Warner Brothers productions when the United Artists Collection was established. Recent events, however, have created at least some doubt in this area. Late in 1977, Warners donated collections consisting of the company's production records and distribution records to the University of Southern California and Princeton University respectively. The precise contents of the collections are not known, since at the present time they are not generally open to scholars. To the best of our knowledge, all extant scripts have been considered in the preparation of these volumes. Should any other versions be discovered at a later date, we will recognize them in future printings of any volumes so affected.

Tino Balio
General Editor

Introduction
The Wax Museum Mystery

Richard Koszarski

Barely two weeks before its scheduled west coast premiere, executives at Warner Brothers ordered a title change on their latest Technicolor production. Originally developed as "The Wax Works" and shot under the title "Wax Museum," the film was now to be known as *Mystery of the Wax Museum*.[1] Title changes are hard to second-guess, but the reason for calling this particular film a "mystery" reveals something special about the Warner Brothers studio and about the image it hoped to create in the minds of its audiences.

In the season of 1932–33, it was clear that the relatively young horror film genre had gone beyond its origins at Universal City, home base of Dracula and Frankenstein. Paramount ventured into pseudoscience with *Island of Lost Souls*; Fox conjured the magical powers of *Chandu, the Magician*; MGM exploited the "realism" of carnival exhibits in *Freaks*; RKO offered the nightmarish fantasy of *King Kong*. And poverty row was not far behind, either.

But at Warner Brothers, Darryl F. Zanuck was in charge of production, and to his mind the newspaper headline was the proper source of movie material. Since the days of the King Tut curse the supernatural may not have been making headlines, but if audiences demanded the new style of thriller, Warner Brothers

1. *Catalogue of Copyright Entries, Motion Pictures 1912–1939* gives the title as *The Mystery of the Wax Museum* (copyrighted February 3, 1933). But the main title on the print is simply *Mystery of the Wax Museum*, which agrees with an extant copyright renewal certificate and is the title I shall use here. To further complicate matters, the original leader (see figure 1) still bears the working title, "Wax Museum."

might see what it could manage. After all, this was still the age of block booking, and a studio's annual program had to appear as well balanced as possible, particularly in regard to popular genre fashions. But while fashion dictated that Warners produce a horror film, its heart was not really in it. The trappings of the genre might be up there on the screen, and the lobby posters might promise Grand Guignol thrills, but audiences would never be allowed to forget that this was primarily a mystery picture. The forces of reason were to be uppermost here, not the forces of darkness. But this conflict of intention between the film and the image of the film upset viewers at the time and puzzles critics of a later day as well. If this film is a "legendary horror classic," [2] why doesn't it behave like one?

In fact, there had been a faint tradition of twenties-style thrillers at Warner Brothers-First National in the days before Zanuck took charge, a small group of films long forgotten today and not very visible in their own time, either. Although one of the very first all-talking films, Roy Del Ruth's *The Terror* (1928) never proved much of a success and seems to have vanished without a trace. Part of a cycle of "dark house" thrillers modeled on *The Bat* and *The Cat and the Canary*, *The Terror* used all the genre trappings of the clutching-hand thriller and employed a particularly photogenic, hooded villain. Benjamin Christensen, noted European director of *The Mysterious X* and *Witchcraft through the Ages*, directed a trio of these films for the studio in 1928–29: *The Haunted House*, *Seven Footprints to Satan*, and *The House of Horror*. Again we see the conventionalized sliding doors and shadowed passageways and the inevitable revelation that it was not *ghosts* behind it all, but criminals, practical jokers, or eccentric relations. Comedy plays a significant part, adding the sting of ridicule to the final debunkings—"Weren't those people fools for shivering in fear of haunted house spooks," the films seem to say. The audience can thus laugh away its own fears while learning a peculiar lesson for a "horror" film: there are no such things as ghosts.

Although such films were made by other studios as well,[3]

2. Program note, New York Film Festival, 1970.
3. For example, Universal made *The Cat and the Canary* in 1927 as a silent film and again in 1930 as a talkie.

Warner Brothers seems to have produced the largest number, demonstrating a real affinity for this most pragmatic variety of horror film. Indeed, its version of *The Gorilla*, released late in 1930, was among the last of the group, appearing only a few months before *Dracula* demonstrated the dramatic shift in audience tastes that would reject such level-headed twenties thinking and substitute instead a desire to escape into supernatural romance.

But while the supernatural proved to be big box office for the rest of Hollywood, Warner Brothers stubbornly resisted. The John Barrymore vehicles *Svengali* and *The Mad Genius* (both 1931) proved unusual enough, thanks largely to Anton Grot's scenic designs, but they were hardly horrifying and not at all supernatural. Finally the studio produced a pair of horror films manqués in which the requisites of studio style battle continually with the conventions of an alien genre: *Doctor X* and its successor, *Mystery of the Wax Museum*. Only at Warners could such films have been produced, for only there was the strain of newspaper realism powerful enough to yield no quarter in a struggle with the surreal requirements of the horror film.

Forerunners of the Screenplay

Mystery of the Wax Museum was a born sequel, specifically designed to capitalize on the success of Warners' first real venture into the bizarre, *Doctor X*. In that film, Lionel Atwill is the director of a New York scientific institute, and Fay Wray is his daughter. A series of "moon killer" murders have plagued the neighborhood, casting suspicion on various members of the institute. Atwill stages an elaborate psychodrama to reveal the identity of the real killer: Preston Foster, who—with the aid of Max Factor's "synthetic flesh"—turns himself into a murderous gargoyle on nights of the full moon. In an action-filled climax, Fay Wray is rescued from the monster's clutches by Lee Tracy, a newspaper reporter who has been hanging around throughout the picture.

Predictably, a large part of the film is devoted to how this reporter gets his story and helps unravel the mystery. The reporter was the most ubiquitous of Warners' heroes of this period, a free-wheeling investigator with entrée to all levels of society. A studiously working-class type, he is related to the detective but functions within a wider sphere of operations. And most conveniently, his news-gathering activities often prove a useful narrative device for harried screenwriters. Although *Doctor X* includes many of the trappings of the classic horror film—mad scientist, bizarre laboratory experiments, gruesome monster—it is at heart a typical detective/reporter program picture, a common enough variety at the studio during the Zanuck regime. It was trade shown in early July 1932, successfully enough that a follow-up picture was immediately planned.

Studio records show that as early as July 19[4] the west coast was wiring the east coast to perform a copyright search on Charles Belden's unpublished story "The Wax Works."[5] Handled through Fulton Brylawski, a Washington attorney who specialized in such work for various studios, the search turned up no copyright registration, but Brylawski did discover one fact of interest: on February 5, *Film Daily* had announced that Charles Rogers, an independent producer working out of Paramount, had purchased a play by Belden entitled "The Wax Museum." Without waiting for Brylawski's findings, however, the studio paid Belden one thousand dollars for his story on July 22 (clearly annoying the executives in New York).

In fact, Rogers had only obtained an option on the property but dropped it when a copyright infringement suit was threatened by Ralph Murphy, co-author of the Broadway play *Black Tower*. In that play (originally entitled "Murdered Alive"), a mad sculptor turns his victims into statues by injecting them with embalming fluid. Although this was the only similarity between the two works, Warners' New York legal staff was cautious, particularly since Rogers and *his* lawyers had concluded the Belden story

4. Interoffice communication (coast wire) from Miss Weiss to Mr. Ebenstein, July 19, 1932. All the studio documents referred to here are from the Warner Brothers legal files of the Wisconsin Center for Film and Theater Research.

5. Charles Belden, formerly a reporter on the *Syracuse Post-Standard*, had been around Hollywood as a screenwriter since 1931. His film career was unimpressive, its highpoint probably being a series of Charlie Chan pictures for Fox in the mid thirties, notably *Charlie Chan at the Opera*. He married actress Joan Marsh in 1938 and died in the Motion Picture County Hospital on November 3, 1954, at the age of fifty. See his obituary in *Variety*, November 10, 1954.

probably was an infringement of *Black Tower* and so had dropped their option. Ralph E. Lewis, a studio attorney, wrote Morris Ebenstein in the New York office that "Zanuck of the studio says that we are really just going to use the title, *The Wax Museum*, and write a complete original story around such title, though at the same time using a few ideas from the original manuscript."[6] Lewis felt justified in assuming that the idea of humans as wax figures was not original with *Black Tower*, but the east coast still felt the situation was "full of potential dynamite."[7]

All this time the studio had been preparing various treatments and the film was nearing production. After comparing the shooting script (probably the version dated September 1, 1932) with a script of "Murdered Alive" as well as with Belden's story, Lewis reported his first conclusion to Ebenstein: the story had not been rewritten at all and "the studio script is almost identical with Belden's story, except for a change of scene from London to New York, and a change of dialogue from upper class British to American newspaper English." But while there were "striking similarities of basic plot" between the material owned by Warners and the play by Murphy, the working out of this plot seemed materially different. "*The Wax Museum* is a newspaper story and *Murdered Alive* is strictly a horror proposition," he wrote. The degree of difference seemed comforting to the studio attorney, who also cited Thorne Smith's popular novel *Night Life of the Gods* as further precedent for the idea of turning people into statues. But ultimately he left any decision on the matter up to the New York office. "There is a closer analogy between these two scripts than there was between *Wings* and *The Dawn Patrol* and we only got clear on *The Dawn Patrol* by the skin of our teeth," he concluded.[8] Available records are silent on the outcome of this predicament, but it would be surprising if Murphy had been able to make the vague similarities between *Black Tower* and *Mystery of the Wax Museum* convincing in a court of arbitration.

6. Lewis to Ebenstein, August 11, 1932.
7. Ebenstein to Lewis, September 1, 1932.
8. Lewis to Ebenstein, September 21, 1932.

The Story Outline

The existing outlines, synopses, and treatments of the film that was to become *Mystery of the Wax Museum* (hereafter cited as *MWM*) can be divided for purposes of study into three groups: (1) the original Belden story outline dated January 3, 1932, which was during the period that Belden was first peddling the story to Rogers or any other interested producer; (2) an initial screen treatment by Don Mullaly and a revision of this treatment by Carl Erickson, both written in July 1932, immediately after Warners acquired the property; and (3) five more treatments written in collaboration by Mullaly and Erickson in August and September 1932, treatments that represent the "Americanized" version of the story as it was eventually filmed.

The Belden original, registered for protection of literary rights on January 4, 1932, seems as close as we can come to the original source of the film. A twelve-page narrative written in scenario form, the text sketches out in general terms a story, some characters, and a few locales. No attempt is made to present it as a finished film with dialogue, camera directions, or even actor suggestions; it is only a skeleton on which a hopeful producer might decide to set a crew of writers to work.

The action opens in 1918 at the waxworks of Mme. Taussaud [*sic*]. Ivan Igor, the attendant and lecturer, is leading a group around the galleries; it is clear that the figure of Marie Antoinette holds a particular fascination for him. That night a fire breaks out, destroying the museum and presumably Igor as well. In 1931 a group of American tourists are engaged in a Cook's Tour of London. Florence Loring and her maiden aunt, Miss Ogglethorpe, are among the group, and love seems to blossom between Florence and their English guide, Rodney Baron. On the itinerary is a visit to the site of the old wax museum, since rebuilt. The newspapers have recently been publicizing a series of mysterious disappearances, and the museum has been enterprising enough to have models of the missing persons on display soon afterward. After closing time, we see a mysterious cloaked figure, a heavy scarf covering the face, who prowls about the exhibits and descends to a subterranean laboratory. When he removes his cloak and scarf, we see that he "has practically no forehead—it being a shriveled, bald pate of seared skin and bone that recedes to a pointed cranium."

Florence tells Rodney that she plans to interview Lady Durham, England's most famous suffragette. Meanwhile, the monster abducts Sir Cecil, a distinguished military authority. Scotland Yard is baffled, and Rodney would like to try to solve the case. While Florence interviews Lady Durham, the monster appears and anesthetizes the suffragette as Florence faints dead away. The monster "sees" Florence garbed in the costume of Marie Antoinette and attempts to carry away both women but has to leave Florence behind when discovered. From a newspaper account, he learns the whereabouts of Florence, but as he is scampering over the rooftops toward her hotel he sees Rodney on guard in the street below and quickly retreats.

By now suspicious of the museum, Rodney prevails on the police to investigate, but they find nothing. Returning with a tour group the next day, Rodney notices some dead flies at the foot of the new statue of Sir Cecil; he collects them in a matchbox and sends them to the police lab, which later reports that the flies were poisoned by formaldehyde, a chemical used in embalming.

The monster finally succeeds in abducting Florence and carries her over the rooftops to his lair, where he reveals both his plan to immortalize her as Marie Antoinette and his identity as Ivan Igor. He displays the corpse of Lady Durham, waiting to be embalmed and cast in wax. Rodney and the police reenter the museum, discover human skin beneath the wax veneer of Sir Cecil's statue, and begin to search the museum. In a struggle with the monster, Florence rips away his scarf, revealing the scarred face underneath, "a blot of drawn, seared, hairless skin—lipless, noseless, and the incarnation of horror." He begins to work feverishly on his preparations for embalming. As he holds the corpse of Lady Durham over a boiling vat of wax, the police break into the underground chamber and shoot; the monster shrieks and falls back into the vat. Rodney and Florence get married on the reward money.

It is surprising that Warners' attorneys should have worried so much about *Black Tower* and missed the more obvious parallels to *The Phantom of the Opera*. The unmasking scene in particular is direct plagiarism, and even the descriptions of the monster's face recall the make-up of Lon Chaney in the 1925 film. There is also an unmistakable flavor of *The Phantom* in the descriptions of the monster's lair, shadowed and dank, set underneath not an opera house but a wax museum. A raving madman during the entire period after he is burned, the monster exhibits violent rages and flights of aesthetic fancy—as in the wonderfully melodramatic "immortal" speech—that are still further recollections of *The Phantom.*

Before leaving the subject of plagiarism, it is worth pointing out that one of the strangest ideas here—the flies poisoned in formaldehyde—turns up in an odd little RKO picture released some two months before *MWM.* In *Secrets of the French Police,* Gregory Ratoff has also been embalming humans and turning them into statues. Finally the hero grows suspicious, finds those dead flies, and sweeps them into a matchbox for later analysis! Even more unusual than this coincidence is the sudden abandonment of this plot thread—the audience never finds out why he collected those flies or what they signified. Not until I read Belden's original story of "The Wax Works" did the action make any sense to me at all. As it happens, the fly incident is left out of the Warners film, but the other similarities are still rather strong. In a review of *MWM,* Martin Dickstein wrote in the *Brooklyn Daily Eagle,* "This is not a new idea in horror pictures. We remember having seen something of the sort several months ago in a murder mystery film whose title we have forgotten." *Secrets of the French Police,* no doubt? With Belden's manuscript circulating around Hollywood in early 1932, some writers at RKO must have seen it, absorbed the wax figure business, and incorporated it into *French Police.* Certainly the acknowledged sources of that film contain no such incident. With the need for hundreds of new features every year, such borrowing was inevitable and kept teams of Hollywood lawyers gainfully employed over the years.

But while such hairline similarities may have concerned Warners' attorneys, they seem of small importance today. We see a clumsy, poorly developed fiction, an idea of some promise but little originality. That it could grow into the screenplay reprinted here—and into the stylishly fashioned film directed by Michael Curtiz—is no small accomplishment.

Mullaly's Treatment

Don Mullaly was the first writer at Warners to attempt a screen adaptation. Born into a theatrical family in St. Louis, Missouri, in 1888, he appeared in vaudeville and on the legitimate stage and began to have some success as a playwright in the mid twenties. His first produced play, *Conscience*, was soon followed by *Laugh That Off*, *The Camels Are Coming*, *Desert Flower*, and other plays. At this time he built and operated an experimental theater in Woodstock, New York. In July 1932 he left for Hollywood under contract to Warner Brothers, and *MWM* appears to have been his first assignment. It seems possible that ill health was the reason for his emigration to a warmer climate, since he entered a tuberculosis sanatorium early in 1933 and died there on April 1. According to his obituary in *Variety*,[9] his screen career included two "originals," *MWM* and *The Blue Moon Murder Mystery* (released as *Girl Missing*), both of which he worked on with Carl Erickson, and adaptations of *She Had to Say Yes* and *Paris Racket*.

On July 27 Mullaly submitted the initial screen treatment of "Wax Works." Not only have Belden's ideas been fleshed out, but a number of significant changes have been introduced as well. Now Igor is no mere attendant but the actual sculptor of the figures. As he takes visitors around his gallery, the art critics Rasmussen and Golatily arrive to praise his work. Igor is particularly fond of Marie Antoinette, whom he addresses as "my wife." In fact, his dead wife had posed for the figure. Golatily has carelessly tossed away a lighted cigarette, and later that night the smoldering butt starts a fire that destroys the museum; Igor barely escapes through a sewer grating.

The Cook's Tour idea is dropped. Instead, Rodney meets Flor-

9. *Variety*, April 11, 1933. His name appears two ways—Mullaly and Mullally—on the covers of the various versions of the screenplay. The *Variety* obituary spells it Mullally; the *Catalogue of Copyright Entries*, Mullaly. I shall spell the name the way it appears on the print of the film: Mullaly.

ence in the lobby of the St. Regis hotel. They had been childhood sweethearts, but a quarrel between their families parted them. Rodney notes the reopening of the wax museum by his best friend, Ivan Igor. The two arrive at the museum to lend a hand and are met by the kindly and well-mannered Igor, who is now confined to a wheelchair.

At the morgue, one of the "corpses" stirs and sits up—its face is monstrous and misshapen.[10] The creature overpowers a guard who discovers him, slips one of the corpses out the window to a pair of confederates waiting in a skiff on the Thames below, and makes good his escape. Back in an underground sanctum, we see the monster preparing a bath of molten wax for his new acquisition and learn that he is Igor, horribly disfigured after the fire and now filling his museum with waxen corpses stolen from morgues. When he suggests kidnapping and murdering Sir Cecil to fill out the collection, his Cockney assistant, Herbert, is terrified. Later, Igor encounters Sir Cecil in a park and asks if he could sculpt his likeness.

The next time the lovers appear at the museum, Igor seems disturbed and sends them away—the similarity to Marie Antoinette has occurred to him. As the monster, he climbs the walls of Florence's hotel in an attempt to abduct her, but her screams frighten him away. Chased by the police and townspeople, he escapes through the sewers. Herbert flees to the countryside in order to avoid involvement in Sir Cecil's impending murder; Rodney and Florence are also in the country, having arranged a family meeting designed to calm their parents' feud. The monster appears on the grounds but is unsuccessful again in abducting Florence. Back in London, he hides in the back seat of Sir Cecil's car and chloroforms him as he enters; he sees the peer as a prospective new Richelieu.

Rodney sees mysterious lights at the museum and has the police search it, but they find nothing. Herbert hears of Sir Cecil's disappearance and returns to London to tell the police what he knows. Rodney learns the truth from Herbert and goes off to the museum. Florence too has gone to the museum in search of Rodney. Igor

10. This piece of action is lifted directly from *Doctor X*.

leads her downstairs, but when he reveals his mad plan she tears at his face, uncovering the hideous features beneath a waxen mask. Rodney and the police appear just as Igor is about to immortalize the body of Sir Cecil, but the monster, using Florence as a shield, escapes through the sewers. When he reaches the river, he is run over by a police motor launch and sinks beneath the waters.

Mullaly's most significant contribution here lies in making Igor an artist who tries to reconstruct through devious means his artworks destroyed in the earlier fire. Hiding behind the mask, he carries on a seemingly normal life and is no longer the cellar-dwelling creature of the original. The smashing of this mask is considerably more effective dramatically than the mere removal of a scarf. But Mullaly shows us early on that Igor is really the monster, and there is no surprise in the final revelation. The 1953 remake, *House of Wax*, also identifies the sculptor as the monster quite soon, but there it seems that the grotesque face is probably the mask, and we are surprised at the end to learn the opposite.

Erickson's Treatment

Three days later, Carl Erickson submitted an "optional outline," a brief sketch of further ideas and refinements meant to fit around Mullaly's more fully developed treatment. Erickson was probably assigned to the project because he had somewhat more screen-writing experience than Mullaly. He had started at Warners in 1930 as a reader and, after writing a successful original for Chic Sale, landed a position on the scenario staff. A much younger man than Mullaly (he was twenty-four when assigned to "Wax Museum"), he seemed to have a career that was developing well (*Silver Dollar, Fashions of 1934, Black Fury*) when he committed suicide on August 29, 1935.[11]

In his outline, Erickson introduces the idea that the owner of the wax museum sets fire to the building for the insurance. He ties up Igor and leaves him in the burning building, but the sculptor's bonds burn through and he escapes. Years later this owner is

11. *Variety*, September 4, 1935.

operating another wax museum, one that features historical characters who resemble corpses that have recently disappeared from London morgues. We learn that Igor is a charred monster who has been supplying the bodies to his old partner, whom he blackmails over the insurance fraud. But the partner recoils from Igor's latest venture, the murder of Sir Cecil.

Rodney, a medical student, is suspicious of the new acquisitions at the museum and takes Florence, his fiancée, to see the figures. The monster sees her from behind a curtain and realizes she is the image of Marie Antoinette. Rodney collects some dead flies from the base of one of the statues and, analyzing them later in the medical school lab, realizes they have died of formaldehyde poisoning. He takes the police to the museum, where they discover human bodies under the wax surfaces.

Meanwhile, Igor murders his partner, arranging the death to look like suicide. The dead man will be blamed for Cecil's murder, and Igor can continue on the trail of Marie Antoinette. He succeeds in abducting Florence from her hotel and evades the police in a chase through London. Back in his underground chamber, he prepares to immortalize Florence, but Rodney and the police appear with the same results as earlier, "and a tag scene with Rodney and Florence in which Rodney begs her to forgive him from preventing her becoming immortal. Florence is glad to be just an ordinary housewife."

Here Igor has once again been reduced to the level of a raging gargoyle, and the fascinating notion of his masked identity has (temporarily) been eliminated. But Erickson did contribute a few ideas that would stay in the picture, notably a detective-story reason for the destruction of the museum and the existence of the museum owner as a second villain. He also understood that it was far better dramatically to have Florence threatened with immortality at the climax than to have her looking on while some secondary corpse is menaced. Erickson shifts our attention away from the lovers and concentrates on the villains, although his substitution of two characters for the interesting dual identity in Mullaly's version is not handled well. The two conceptions would be fused in the next treatment.

Introduction

Mullaly-Erickson Treatments

Mullaly and Erickson were now assigned to work on the project as a team, and within ten days they produced a substantially different treatment, one that not only Americanized the material but quite definitely Warnerized it as well.[12] We do not know who suggested the direction of these changes, although one of the Lewis letters quoted earlier implies that the idea came from Zanuck himself.

In this version, critics Rasmussen and Golatily visit Ivan Igor in his London wax museum, praising the beauty of his exhibits, particularly the Marie Antoinette. After they leave, Igor's partner, George Wells, arrives and announces that he plans to burn down the museum for the fire insurance. Igor protests, but Wells torches the exhibits and knocks him unconscious; with the building in flames, Igor barely escapes through a sewer grating.

The action shifts to the offices of the *New York Times* on New Year's Eve, 1932. The editor berates Florence, a fun-loving reporter, for failing to bring in any hot news and gives her four hours to return with a story. A scene with Wells shows him on the telephone, arranging a suspicious truck delivery. In the morgue, a hideous-looking monster selects a corpse and passes it out the window to someone waiting outside. Later, a group of truckers, including a sniveling Cockney named Sparrow, deliver a mysterious crate to Wells.

At the police station, Florence receives a tip about the Joan Gale autopsy and goes off to the morgue where the police discover the Gale body is missing. Florence has her story. They arrest Harold

12. The first of the Mullaly and Erickson treatments, labeled "Second Detailed Outline," is dated August 5 on page 1 but August 9 on the title page. There is no writer credit, although the names Erickson, Mullaly, and Blanke are written in pencil below the title. Henry Blanke was the production supervisor at Warners assigned to the film. His early experience was with the German UFA company, and he came to America with Ernst Lubitsch. He had supervised Warners' German productions (1928–30) and foreign language Burbank productions (1930–31) before becoming one of the studio's regular staff of production supervisors. He was not a writer, and his name on the cover may simply indicate that he is also to receive a mimeograph copy.

Winton, the dead woman's playboy lover, and charge him with complicity in the disappearance. Florence interviews Winton in jail and feels he is being railroaded. Back at the paper, she tells this to her editor, connecting the event to six other similar disappearances.

The London Wax Museum is about to open in New York. Igor is the proprietor, and he directs a staff of artists in creating the figures, since he is crippled and can no longer work. Among the crew are Hugo, a deaf and mute "Boris Karloff type," and Ralph, a young medical student apparently earning extra money by working at the museum as a sculptor. Igor criticizes Ralph's work, noting that on one of his figures the forearm is "at least six inches longer" than the other. He accuses Ralph of being a "modernist" and goes on to criticize Hugo's work, bemoaning his inability to create the figures himself. Sparrow arrives with a large crate, which contains the "strangely lifelike" figure of a seated woman; Igor praises his artistic style.

Ralph calls his girlfriend, Charlotte, and arranges a luncheon date with her and her roommate, Florence. Winton is released on bail. In a cab, Florence pokes fun at Charlotte "for her interest in the penniless student." When they arrive at the museum, Igor is startled to see that Charlotte resembles his Marie Antoinette and tells her so. After lunch the girls walk home, and Igor, under the pretext of asking Charlotte to pose, learns from Ralph that the girls live on Commerce Street. Sparrow and Hugo smile suspiciously.

Back at the office, Florence tells her editor that one of the wax figures she saw on her visit to the museum looks like Gale. Her theory is that Ralph stole the corpse, made a death mask, and later disposed of the body to a group of medical students. She telephones Winton and asks to see him later.

That night the monster appears on the fire escape outside Charlotte's window, but, just as he is about to enter and kidnap her, Florence arrives. Later at the museum, Florence inspects the suspicious figure and learns from Igor that Sparrow was its creator. With Winton, she follows Sparrow to the building occupied by Wells. When Winton begs off, she enters the building alone. Inside she discovers a mysterious pine box and catches a glimpse of the monster. She convinces Winton and a passing policeman that something strange is going on, and the police seize Sparrow, who has just come out the door after a meeting with Wells. Both Wells and the monster are inside as the police break in but find nothing except a case of Scotch.

At the police station, Sparrow gets the third degree; the police expect to get some answers out of him because he is "a junky." Florence arrives at the station and is introduced to a man from Scotland Yard who is in New York investigating the disappearance eighteen months earlier of Sir Cecil, some of whose jewelry has turned up in a local pawnshop. Florence immediately connects the case with her own. A pawnbroker identifies Sparrow as the source of the jewelry. Rushing back to the newspaper (fending off a marriage proposal on the way), Florence locates in the files a picture of Sir Cecil.

Early next morning the police are still questioning Sparrow, while Charlotte, searching for Ralph, appears at the wax museum. Igor asks her in to see a new shipment of miniatures, and she helps him down to his workroom. Suddenly he leaps from the chair and seizes her, babbling that he has found his Marie Antoinette. Terrified, she strikes at his face, revealing that of the monster under a waxen mask. Upstairs, Ralph arrives as Florence and Winton drive up. While Winton finds a parking space, Florence enters the museum and compares the picture of Sir Cecil to one of the statues ("probably Voltaire"). Below, Igor is raving and shows Charlotte the embalmed body of Wells on whom he has finally avenged himself. Her screams are heard upstairs, and the group begins searching for her. Meanwhile, Sparrow finally confesses the facts about the museum to the police. Ralph finds the monster's chamber but is quickly knocked out; Winton hesitates going down but blocks the monster's exit. As the police arrive, the monster "gives one final scream of defiance and hurls his body over the railing, whirling downward into one of the boiling vats." Florence and Winton race uptown to her newspaper, and when she arrives she receives—and accepts—a surprising proposal of marriage from her editor.

With this treatment, Mullaly and Erickson had changed the film (in the words of one Warners attorney) from "strictly a horror proposition" to something much more congenial. Suddenly the film is a New York newspaper story, and a new character, the reporter, comes to dominate the action. The film is no longer the horror proposition of villain versus lovers but the detective situation of villain versus investigator. It has the slangy flavor of a Cagney picture and the up-to-date trappings of Park Avenue playboys, cynical modern maidens, and degenerate immigrant drug addicts. The use of the reporter hero might be part of the decision to copy *Doctor X* as closely as possible, but, as mentioned earlier, this device was relatively common at Warners during the period. That this character is also a woman may reflect the success of Joan Blondell in a similar role in *Miss Pinkerton* (1932), but in fact the woman as efficient working girl was also characteristic of Warners in those days.

Mullaly and Erickson produced several more drafts of this version in August and September before submitting the "final shooting script" of September 22, which is reprinted here. In annotating this script, I have indicated the minor changes introduced in the intermediate treatments of August 11, August 22, and September 1 and noted the differences between the final screenplay and the completed film, which in some cases are fairly significant.

Cast and Technical Staff

In line with the desire to copy as closely as possible the style and substance of *Doctor X*, Warners not only assembled the same creative team behind the camera but also brought back some of the original cast, notably Lionel Atwill and Fay Wray.

Atwill, born in England in 1885, had appeared on stage opposite Nazimova, Katharine Cornell, and Helen Hayes. *Doctor X* was his second major Hollywood role and led to his being typed as villain or obsessed hero in several more macabre films. Substantial roles in *Song of Songs, Nana,* and *The Devil Is a Woman* could never overcome the image established by *The Vampire Bat, Murders in the Zoo, Mark of the Vampire,* and numerous other horror films.

Fay Wray had been rescued from Universal westerns by her featured role in von Stroheim's *The Wedding March* and had worked for Stiller, von Sternberg, and Capra. After *Doctor X*, she appeared again opposite Atwill in *The Vampire Bat* (for Majestic, a poverty-row outfit); *MWM* was their third film together.[13] Although in production earlier, *King Kong* would not appear until a month after *MWM*.

Familiar Warners contract players Glenda Farrell and Frank McHugh were new additions, playing the roles of reporter and editor that were added to the script after it had been Americanized. Farrell had experience in stock and on Broadway before coming to Warners in 1930. While the studio kept her busy with various supporting roles, notably in *Little Caesar* and *I Am a Fugitive from a Chain Gang*, it shied away from featuring her in more important productions. If a wise-cracking blonde was needed to play opposite Cagney, Joan Blondell would probably get the nod; Farrell's image seemed just a little too hard boiled. Even here she is billed beneath Fay Wray, whose part amounts to little more than a guest appearance. In the late thirties, she continued her characterization of the fast-talking lady reporter in a series of Torchy Blane B pictures, also for Warners.

Frank McHugh was another veteran of the studio stock company, like Farrell joining up in 1930 after a career on the stage. A fine supporting player, he made notable appearances in such films as *The Dawn Patrol*, *The Crowd Roars*, and *The Dark Horse*. But his part here seems almost an afterthought, an attempt to supply a foil for the girl reporter the studio had introduced into the script. All of his scenes take place inside his office, a strategy that might be efficient in terms of production management (he appeared in at least fifteen films in 1933) but does tend to cut him off from the rest of the action.[14] The very fact that *MWM* ends with inveterate supporting players Farrell and McHugh in a clinch is proof that this film is not to be considered one of the season's more important releases.

13. Among the supporting players, Arthur Edmund Carewe was also brought back from the cast of *Doctor X*, again in the role of a red-herring villain.

14. One critic wrote recently that McHugh seems so disconnected from the proceedings that he "looks as if he had just walked over from a Walsh picture on the next lot" (Robert Mundy, "Death Plays and Wax Works," *Cinema* [London], no. 9, p. 8).

As *Doctor X* was filmed in Technicolor so was *MWM*, and Ray Rennahan and his camera operator, Dick Towers, were again supplied by the Technicolor Corporation to photograph it. Earlier Warners Technicolor films had been photographed by their own contract cinematographers (such as Barney McGill, Dev Jennings, Lee Garmes), occasionally in association with a Technicolor man like Rennahan. But *Doctor X* and *MWM* were shot by Rennahan alone. By not assigning one of its own people to work with Rennahan, the studio may have been demonstrating faith in his abilities, or it may have considered these projects not important enough to waste a second cinematographer on them.

After this film, Rennahan went on to photograph a series of Technicolor shorts for the studio, but *MWM* appears to have been the last significant film shot in two-color Technicolor, a red and green process incapable of reproducing the full range of the spectrum. First popularized in the mid twenties mainly for special insert sequences, the process achieved its greatest success in the early sound years as a means of photographing musicals. Warners had an exceptionally heavy commitment to the process, and *Gold Diggers of Broadway*, *Golden Dawn*, and *Viennese Nights* were among the pre-Berkeleyan Technicolor musicals filmed there. By 1931 the public was losing interest, and outright hostility greeted the appearance of *MWM* in 1933.

The introduction of a three-color process in 1934 finally made natural color features practicable, and public interest gradually revived; but in 1933 audiences and critics seemed disinterested and even dismayed. In retrospect, the unnatural pastel hues of two-color Technicolor were well suited to such stylized genres as the musical or the horror film, and *MWM* used the pale reds, not-quite blues, and garish greens in nearly expressionist fashion. Unfortunately, it proved impossible to copy the dye-transfer color of this film onto modern color-negative stock. According to film archivist and historian William K. Everson, available 16mm copies were made "as cheaply and with as little effort as possible, thus robbing the film of its one major asset, its rich and often creative pastel coloring. In the prints that have since been made for television use, the film looks almost like a black and white film, *artificially* colored; single tones—blues or ambers—tending to dominate for whole reels at a time." [15] The prints examined for this study were equally degraded, with shades of brown and green dominant. The imaginative palette displayed in the original copy is no longer to be seen, and the color design bears no relationship to it whatsoever. [16]

Settings were again the product of Anton Grot, head of the Warners art department. Originally Antocz Franciszek Groszewski, he was born in Poland and studied art in Cracow and Königsberg. Always at his best with exotic or even bizarre material, he was Oscar-nominated for *Svengali* in 1931; *The Walking Dead* and *A Midsummer Night's Dream* would later be among his most striking creations. His designs for *MWM* are clearly similar to the work he did on *Doctor X*, even to the extent of reusing some of the laboratory equipment (for example, the plastic nozzle of Igor's wax machine was originally part of the elaborate lie detector in *Doctor X*). Of his work on *Doctor X*, he said at the time, "When we design a set for mystery and melodrama we know that it must be of heavy construction with dark colorings and shadows. When we want to add menace to that, we put in a top-heavy effect over doors and windows, we build in low arches which give the feeling of overhanging danger. We design a set that imitates as closely as possible a bird of prey about to swoop down upon its victim, trying to incorporate in the whole thing a sense of impending calamity, of overwhelming danger." [17]

Many of Grot's finest films were directed by Michael Curtiz, a Hungarian who shared Grot's baroque, eastern European sensibility. Known as a director of spectacles in Europe, Curtiz arrived at Warners at the close of the silent era and quickly became one of the studio's workhorses (it released seven of his films in 1933). He was one of the few emigres to blend successfully the stylized mood

15. William K. Everson, *Classics of the Horror Film* (Secaucus, N.J.: Citadel Press, 1974), p. 105.

16. Reviewing the original print as screened at the New York Film Festival, I was clearly under the spell of the "outstanding," "magnificent," and "strikingly modern" color scheme (Richard Koszarski, "Lost and Found," *Film Comment* [Spring, 1971], pp. 71–72).

17. From the *Doctor X* press book, as quoted in Donald Deschner, "Anton Grot: Warners Art Director 1927–1948," *The Velvet Light Trap*, no. 15 (Fall, 1975), p. 19.

of European visuals with the rapid-fire pacing more typical of American films, as *MWM* so well shows. While the producers and writers did their best to Americanize the material, Curtiz consciously resurrected the principles of German expressionist film making to enhance the "intangible feeling of uneasiness" at the core of the work. Curtiz spoke of his visual style through an interview for the press book of *MWM*:

Odd, unusual camera angles should never be used for their own sake though the temptation to do so is often great, especially to the man who has an aptitude for thinking in them. The only reason for using an angle, in presenting a scene that would not seem the usual one to the onlooker, is to obtain a definite effect upon the spectator, which can be gained in no other way. You wish to arouse at that point a feeling of surprise, of terror, of repulsion, of admiration—and to emphasize it, the person or thing you are photographing must be presented from a special angle. Otherwise the natural, straightforward method of recording a scene in pictures is the one that holds the spectator's interest, keeps the story moving and preserves the flow and tempo of the action. It is very easy, in a story like *The Mystery of the Wax Museum*, for instance, to overdo the use of bizarre, startling angles. That is why I used them throughout the picture sparingly, and always with a definite purpose in mind. Unless one is chary of the employment of them, their effect is very quickly blunted, and thereafter they become a nuisance instead of a help. Much more effective is the specialized type of lighting we used to establish and build up a mood that we wished to communicate with the spectator. This was particularly true of the sequences laid in the two wax works—the London one and the New York museum. In each, without being too obvious in our lighting, we tried to arouse in the spectators' minds a vague, intangible feeling of uneasiness, mystery, a sinister something lurking in the shadows, never shown but only suggested. The use of color is an asset in creating such moods in a story of this type. To be sure, stories of the fantastic, the horrible, the bizarre have been told with fullest success in black and white photography. But it has always been a question in my mind whether those very stories would not have been more gripping, more realistic, if they had been photographed in color such as we have employed with such unusual success in *The Mystery of the Wax Museum* and previously in *Dr. X*.[18]

18. Press book, *Mystery of the Wax Museum*, from the Theatre Collection of the New York Public Library.

Clearly, while directing a film every six weeks, Curtiz had little or nothing to say about the scripts assigned to him. Even on so important a film as *Casablanca*, the final script was not yet completed by the time the shooting began. Such working conditions forced him into unusually imaginative manipulations of the mise en scène, not only in the selection of angles and lighting described here but also in a breakdown of shots often far different than that described in the script.

The last important member of the technical staff of *Doctor X* repeating here was film editor George Amy, just at the beginning of a long career with Warners. He would come to be associated with Curtiz and Berkeley, and eventually he left editing to become a producer and director himself.

But the connections between the two films are undoubtedly even broader than these, for with all these credited talents must have come a host of anonymous assistants, an extended family carefully reassembled by the studio to duplicate their success of the previous season.

Promotion

Although *MWM* was part of the regular Warners' program, and as such was sold to exhibitors in a block along with other more or less desirable productions, it was necessary to help the exhibitor sell the picture to *his* audience. To this end, each release was provided with a press book, an almanac of technical information, available advertising art, stories to plant in local newspapers, and often wacky publicity stunts intended to capture the widest possible audience.

The press book issued for *MWM* contains the usual run of poster illustrations, biographies of prominent cast members, and anecdotal ephemera relating to the production (for example, a special heat-resistant wax was used to protect the figures from the studio lights, although the forty mannequins burned up in the fire were "doubles" created in the usual fashion). How far such press releases can be trusted is open to question, although the technical material is usually more convincing than the biographical "facts." Exhibitors are exhorted to open a wax museum of their own in the theater lobby, and sources of supply are indicated. In fact, at the film's west coast premiere, the actual mannequins used in the film were put on display in the lobby of the Hollywood theater.[19]

Of major interest here, however, is a rather revealing pep talk intended to emphasize the film's most salable points and skirt gently around weak or troublesome areas. This general introduction baldly exposes the studio's own attitude toward the film, its strengths and its weaknesses:

Suspense is the keynote of your campaign on *The Mystery of the Wax Museum*, with the novelty production idea secondary but still vitally important.

By "novelty production idea," the studio means the horror film overtones. Emphasizing "suspense," instead of, say, "shock," pushes the film more firmly into the mystery genre and away from the horror mold.

To be sold effectively, the theme must be emotionalized to the utmost. You are not dealing with wax figures—but with one decidedly human and dominating character who has surrounded himself with lovely creatures WHO MAY BE WOMEN OR WHO MAY BE WAX. Get that question over—"Women or Wax?" Plant it solidly in the minds of your patrons and DON'T TELL THEM THE ANSWER!

The fear that audiences would reject films based solely on gimmicks clashed with a compulsion to employ these gimmicks in the first place. Emphasizing the star and his "decidedly human" situation was the solution here—although one would have to strain to see this as the dominant element of the film. The "women or wax" motif, while it certainly can be traced to the film, is exaggerated mightily in order to get some sex into the campaign. In line with this, much of the ad art featured Atwill molding the torso of a grotesquely proportioned amazon (for example, the still photo, taken for publicity purposes, that is used on the cover of this volume).

Capitalize on the popularity of *Dr. X* by pointing up the fact that *The Mystery of the Wax Museum* was made by the same director with the same star team. In Atwill, Wray, McHugh and Farrell you have four names of

19. *Los Angeles Times*, February 8, 1933.

recognized drawing power. Sell them! Of course the TECHNICOLOR feature should be displayed in everything you do.

That first line is admirably auteurist, although one wonders how many exhibitors were prepared to exploit this as a Michael Curtiz film! The position of the film as a sequel to *Doctor X* is made explicit, but the drawing power of the cast is another question. According to the canny estimate of *Variety*, the film had "no wow marquee value." [20] The half-hearted mention of Technicolor indicates the low estate to which this process had fallen, and elsewhere we learn that the film is also available in black and white.

Pick the angles best suited to the local situation for emphasis. While *The Mystery of the Wax Museum* is distinctly a mystery picture, the clowning of Farrell and McHugh is one of the big elements and can stand a heavy play if you want to appeal to the laugh fans. Some of the ad art is "stronger" than others. You know best what type will be acceptable to your public.

Not a word so far about thrills or shocks. Instead, exhibitors are encouraged to try selling it as a comedy if they feel a mystery will not go over. And the reference to the sleazy character of the ads is one last admission that, if all else fails, you can always sell the picture on sex.

The Critics

But the critics (and audiences?) were not about to be lulled into submission by a lobby decorated with waxworks. By February of 1933, a reaction against horror films had set in, and, although Warners worked overtime to stress the film's nonhorror qualities, the words *macabre, shock,* and *horror* filled nearly every review.

"If you still like horror films it may interest you," wrote John S. Cohen in the *New York Sun*, and with characteristic hindsight *Variety*'s Abel saw a connection between the film's style and its arrival at the end of a cycle. "*Wax Museum* would have been certain of better gate support a year ago," he wrote. "Recognizing this, the Technicolor and the hyper-weirdness apparently were mandatory studio precautions to offset the element of belated arrival." How the studio was to have predicted the demise of the genre in time to

20. Abel, *Variety*, February 21, 1933.

decide on filming it in Technicolor is left unanswered, as is the entire question of Technicolor's box-office value in the first place.

Even from those critics who did not admit to writing off all horror films in advance, any number of elements were found lacking. Thornton Delehanty of the *New York Evening Post* felt that the film "never achieves anything but a wax-like imitation of horror. The newspaper scenes are filled with painfully unfunny dialogue, so that even such good actors as Glenda Farrell and Frank McHugh are made to seem bad. The picture, incidentally, is photographed in Technicolor, which leaves it about where it would have been in black and white." Likewise, the *New York American* labeled it "absurd and tedious" but at least found the time to praise director Curtiz. Consistently attacked was the "loose and unconvincing story,"[21] which was thought "a bit clumsily plotted."[22] Significantly, at least one reviewer was annoyed by genre mixing: "Connoisseurs of mystery fiction may well despise *The Mystery of the Wax Museum* because it breaks the rule that everything must be explained at the finish," wrote *Time*'s critic. Apparently taking this "mystery" at its word, he misses the heroine's gathering all the principals together at the conclusion in order to unravel the plot threads for the audience, a convention of "dark house" thrillers, perhaps, but not straight horror films.

Finally, the effect of the stylization achieved by Curtiz and Grot was found unacceptable by more than one critic. "Its artificiality is uncompromising, consequently there is little sympathetic appeal or the least relation to reality,"[23] wrote the *Los Angeles Times*, and again for *Variety*, "The studious cynicism of the [Farrell] character creates a theatrical artificiality." Never is there any effort to understand this artificial style, merely the obligation to condemn it once it has been identified. To balance these, there were few positive appraisals, one of the warmest being a mere two and one-half stars proffered by the *New York Daily News*. The *Los Angeles Times* thought the film's "mechanical devices" were superior to those in *Frankenstein*, even if the film as a whole was "not quite as good."

21. Abel, *Variety.*
22. John S. Cohen, *New York Sun.*
23. *Los Angeles Times*, February 26, 1933.

Introduction

The Film Today

With such a press, it seems hard to believe that the film soon grew into a "legendary horror classic," but this is exactly what happened. Withdrawn from the American market soon after its release and from Europe by the mid forties, *MWM* held a special place in the memories of those who had seen it and for many of those who had not. "The power of its best scenes lingers in the memory after two decades,"[24] wrote Carlos Clarens, while Ivan Butler felt the unmasking scene "is so strong as to leave its impression on the memory after thirty years."[25] While it may be true that absence makes the heart grow fonder, especially in so romantic an area as film history, there must be something more substantial behind this idealized vision of a film that was pretty well panned on its first appearance.

Although *MWM* was dismissed by grown-up critics at the time ("It is not a critic's picture, nor one that invites lengthy analysis,"[26] said the *Los Angeles Times*), its effect on younger viewers may have been more than usually profound. Certainly the psychoanalytic overtones of this fairy story are potent: a falsely benign father figure turns healthy young bodies into wax dolls, preserving them for all time in a static parody of youth and beauty. As Ivan Igor plainly says (in an unnecessary speech wisely cut from the film): "My child, my child, if you will just listen to me, then you will not be afraid. Don't you understand, dear, that I love you? Don't you know that at times when I have wanted to die— I could not die because I had not saved you. And now you are here, to be given, a thing of delight, to all the world. I am trying to grant you immortality."[27]

Seldom do we see even in a horror film so direct an attempt by the father to transform the "child" into the image of the dead mother. While grown-up critics might complain about the film's wobbly dramatic structure, younger viewers had different

24. Carlos Clarens, *An Illustrated History of the Horror Film* (New York: Putnam, 1967), p. 81.
25. Ivan Butler, *The Horror Film* (New York: A. S. Barnes, 1967), p. 13.
26. *Los Angeles Times*, February 26, 1933.
27. Scene 165 in this script.

thoughts on their minds.[28] No wonder that such a film should maintain an inexplicable hold on them twenty or thirty years later, and that the fervor of this fascination should be so easily communicated to those too young to remember the film themselves.

But fantasies rooted at this level are hard to sustain in the face of cold facts, and the film's reception after 1970 was predictable: the magic evaporated while all the flaws of narrative structure and gag writing returned to prominence. Two fairly long assessments are typical. Writing in *Photon*, a journal published for horror and science fiction fans, Ronald V. Borst reports of the film's New York Film Festival screening, "Horror buffs were in profusion, yet when the film concluded the general consensus was that [the] film was less than the legend had built up over the years."[29] For Borst (who apparently had not seen the film earlier), the main disappointment is the film's all-too-obvious position as a sequel to *Doctor X*, which he details through numerous parallels of incident, narrative structure, and style. The "over-abundance of comic interludes" is one of these unfortunate similarities, although he admits that "Glenda Farrell's comic heroine is still quite amusing and . . . can be considered one of the best things the picture offers." He finds her performance superior to that of Lee Tracy in the similar role in *Doctor X* but feels the comedy in both cases subverts the hoped-for "atmosphere." These complaints are fairly similar to those of the original critics, revealing a surprising unanimity of opinion over the years. Ultimately Borst admits that the film's reappearance proves "the end of a glorious legend," a comment that certainly shows the potency of failed expectations. In fact, he rates it only a notch or two above films like *Murders in the Zoo* and *The Vampire Bat*, and distinctly inferior to the remake, *House of Wax*.

While not so devastating, William K. Everson's commentary in *Classics of the Horror Film* is equally disapproving.[30] Everson *had*

28. "This one may serve to chase the sandman from the bedside of the more timid and credulous kiddies, but as a motion picture catering to adult audiences, it is an absurd and tedious film" (*New York American*).

29. Ronald V. Borst, "On Wax Museums and Mysteries," *Photon*, no. 20 (1971), pp. 6–10.

30. Everson, *Classics of the Horror Film*, pp. 104–11.

seen the film earlier but still shares the estimate of the film as a disappointment. His essay explains this feeling with a shrewd description of how a viewer's memory can "redirect" a film over a period of years. But, characteristically, he finds a few isolated elements worthy of praise: the production design of Grot, the performance of Atwill, "the soft hues of the old two-color Technicolor" (p. 108), and the relatively restrained use of the monster itself. In general, he feels it superior to *House of Wax* but distinctly inferior to *Doctor X*. Again, the catalog of liabilities is serious. Not only does the film lack music, but the dramatic structure once more comes under attack. "It is constructed far more as a mystery than as a horror film, with so many characters and sub-plots that too much time is taken away from the basic story line" (p. 106). While more generous than Borst, Everson ruefully agrees that it is "not quite the classic that we remembered" (p. 111).

There were, however, a few favorable opinions. Robert Mundy, again comparing the film to *Doctor X*, felt both films "part of an early high-point to Curtiz's undulating Hollywood career,"[31] although his critique is unfortunately brief. My own critique, written after the New York Film Festival screening, singled out the film's Technicolor photography, production design, and the captivating performance of Glenda Farrell. It seemed to me "one of the few important discoveries of the season, but not for the reasons everyone had expected."[32] More recently the film was the subject of a reappraisal by John Davis, a specialist in the work of director Curtiz.[33] Davis points out Curtiz's addition of suspenseful "search" episodes to the script and generally pictures it as an improvement over *Doctor X*. But most importantly, he refrains from judging it purely in terms of genre and is aware that the overpowering studio style behind *MWM* requires a special frame of critical reference.

In the years since its reappearance, *MWM* has had an uphill

31. Mundy, "Death Plays and Wax Works."

32. Koszarski, "Lost and Found," p. 72.

33. John Davis, "When Will They Ever Learn?" *The Velvet Light Trap*, no. 15 (Fall, 1975), pp. 11–17.

battle to reestablish its once formidable position in film history. At first dismissed for failing to live up to the idealized image of a horror film that never existed, it is slowly gathering a new reputation, based largely on its grand stylistic flourishes and considerable visual wit. For those expecting some sort of James Whale film, *MWM* will always be a disappointment. But viewers who can disabuse themselves of the "glorious legend" have a unique opportunity to witness a test of strength between studio style and genre conventions. *MWM* helps define Warners "realism" by marking its ultimate extreme. Unfortunately, its position on this fringe, with the consequent confusions of style and genre, has aggravated and perplexed two generations of critics. Street-smart New Yorkers spouting thirties aphorisms tangle uneasily with a distinctly eastern European mise en scène. The requisites of a mystery story vie for playing time with the conventions of a horror film. A typical Warner Brothers production dons a fright wig and tries to pass itself off as a Universal picture. For many, the film is nothing but a bundle of conflicts that constantly threaten to pull it to pieces. Yet surely the real mystery behind "Wax Museum" is not only *why* the story was ever filmed but *how* Curtiz and the production people at Warners managed to resolve these conflicts as gracefully as they did.

1. The original leader still carries the film's working title, "Wax Museum."

2. Oblivious to any fire hazard, Ivan Igor (Lionel Atwill) dangles a smoldering cigarette from his lips as he works among the inflammable "children" of his wax museum.

3. *Fay Wray doubles as the original figure of Marie Antoinette.*

4. *One of the special wax figures created by Otis and Campbell substitutes for Fay Wray as Marie Antoinette loses her head in the conflagration scene.*

5. First appearance of "the Monster" amid the domed splendor of Anton Grot's fanciful Bellevue morgue.

6. The dope-dealing action in scene 46 is played completely in shadow.

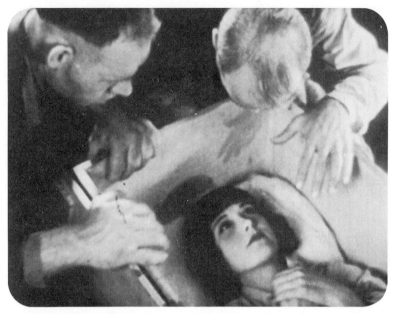

7. *Monica Bannister plays the waxen corpse of Joan Gale, but she is never seen as a live character in the film.*

8. *A pre-Code boudoir scene with Fay Wray and Glenda Farrell absorbs the entire dialogue and action of the taxi scene (scenes 68 and 71).*

9. One of Curtiz's characteristic transition shots introduces the police station for scene 69.

10. From Igor's point of view, Charlotte lap-dissolves into the figure of Marie Antoinette.

11. *Reporter and editor (Glenda Farrell and Frank McHugh)—a relationship of mutual aggravation and affection.*

12. *Perc Westmore's monster make-up. "We were able to create a completely new face . . . which he could vivify at will," he wrote in the press book for the film.*

13. *Curtiz's handling of Grot's plainly expressionist design recalls the feeling of Wiene's* Raskolnikov *and other German classics of a decade earlier.*

14. *The police use third-degree methods on Sparrow, who continually "rubs hand across nose as cocaine fiends are known to do."*

15. *The "horror chamber" beneath the wax museum, one of many surviving echoes of* The Phantom of the Opera.

16. *In the film, Charlotte wanders through a dark maze of tunnels and passageways, a sinister journey only hinted at in the script.*

17. "Igor sweeps Charlotte into his arms . . .

18. Charlotte struggles . . .

17–22. The unmasking scene; frames from consecutive shots.

19. *She tears at Igor's face . . .*

20. *. . . revealing . . .*

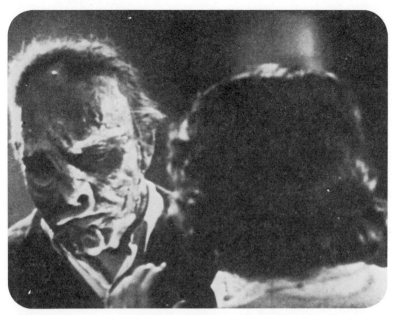

21. . . . the horribly mutilated face of the Monster.

22. Charlotte screams and faints." (scene 156)

Mystery of the Wax Museum

Screenplay
by
DON MULLALY
and
CARL ERICKSON

Mystery of the Wax Museum

FADE IN ON
TITLE: PROLOGUE   LONDON, 1920.[1]

DISSOLVE TO:

1.   INT. MUSEUM OF IVAN IGOR
where he exhibits groups and individuals done in wax.
The figures are of historic characters and events. The place
is almost in darkness as the steel blinds are drawn on the
windows facing the street. Through the back and side
windows we see and hear a pouring rain. At the fade in
we hear the distant rumbling of thunder, and shortly
thereafter there is a blinding flash of lightning through
the unshuttered windows showing in clear relief a brutal,
sinister face, the black hood and cowl suggesting a
medieval monk. We see, lying at the foot of the monkish
figure, a seminude figure of a woman whose back is sadly
lacerated. She is lying face down. In the monk's hand is a
knout or cat-o'-nine-tails, as though he had been pun-
ishing her.

In the background of this shot we see a workbench and
a work light. The vague figure of Igor is seen, at work on a
nearly completed bust. DOLLY UP TO A CLOSE-UP of Igor's
hands. We see that they are the sensitive, fine hands of an
artist, dexterous in their delicate occupation.

CUT TO:

2.   FULL FIGURE OF IGOR
as he steps back from the bench.[2] Evidently satisfied, he
goes to a basin of water and puts his hands in it and stands
as though resting them.

3.   EXT. STREET   LONG SHOT   MUSEUM IN BACKGROUND

It is raining and we see an occasional flash of lightning. The figure of Worth[3] on the opposite side of street from museum, walking rapidly AWAY FROM CAMERA, comes to a point diagonally opposite museum and glances furtively about, starts toward the entrance. When a policeman appears, he darts quickly to a doorway, concealing himself. The officer crosses the street and disappears along an intersecting street.[4] Worth makes a second endeavor to approach the museum, when a hansom cab draws up to the curb and Dr. Rasmussen and Golatily alight and cross the sidewalk toward door. Worth slinks back to his hiding place. The cab draws away.

4.   CLOSE SHOT   GOLATILY AND RASMUSSEN ON STEPS

GOLATILY (glancing at watch):
    A beastly hour to disturb the fellow.

RASMUSSEN:
    Not at all. He works late and he'll be delighted.

They knock at door.[5]

5.   INT. MUSEUM   CLOSE SHOT OF IGOR

washing hands. He straightens up and glances toward door, showing annoyance, then starts toward door. The knock is repeated.

6.   EXT. MUSEUM

Rasmussen is pressing his face to glass, looks through, and we see, through the glass panel of the door, Igor approaching. When he glimpses his visitors, his expression changes from annoyance to one of extreme pleasure, and hastening his stride he opens the door quickly.

IGOR (with slight foreign accent):
    Well, well, my friend, this is an unexpected pleasure.

RASMUSSEN (shaking hands with Igor):
> I shouldn't have thought of disturbing you but it happens the friend I told you of is leaving tomorrow to supervise some new excavations in Egypt, and he was anxious to look at your collection before going away. May I present Mr. Golatily?

IGOR:
> It is a great pleasure. I have heard so much about you.

7.   INT. MUSEUM
The three men enter museum, Igor closing the door and locking it. Igor laughs.

IGOR:
> My children will become conceited that so distinguished a critic has thought them interesting enough to review.

8.   EXT. MUSEUM FROM OPPOSITE SIDE OF STREET
Worth, standing in doorway opposite museum, waiting impatiently.[6]

8A.   INT. MUSEUM
Igor throws light switches, one at a time, each circuit illuminating a different group. He names them as he throws each switch.

IGOR:
> Sidney Carton on the Guillotine.

9.   CLOSE SHOT
of the figure. We hear Golatily's voice.

GOLATILY'S VOICE:
> Very interestingly done.

CAMERA PANS TO figure of Sir Walter Raleigh as the lights are thrown on this figure. We hear Igor's voice.

IGOR'S VOICE:
Sir Walter Raleigh.

RASMUSSEN'S VOICE:
I was particularly interested in this one. See the fineness with which he has mounted that beard.

CAMERA PANS TO figure of Joan d'Arc, as lights are thrown on it and we hear Igor's voice.

IGOR'S VOICE:
Joan d'Arc.[7]

GOLATILY'S VOICE:
It's a pity to race through such an exhibition. One should have time to really study them.

CAMERA PANS TO figure of Voltaire. The lights are thrown on and we hear Igor's voice.

IGOR'S VOICE:
Voltaire.

The two visitors are standing at the moment beside the figure of Voltaire. Golatily backs away from it, half closing his eyes and studying it critically.

GOLATILY:
You could almost expect him to speak. I wonder what he'd say after all these years.

Igor joins them, laughing.

IGOR:
You would be astonished. He is more difficult now, to those in authority, than even the records show. He was a very stubborn person, I assure you.

RASMUSSEN:
Stubborn?

IGOR:
Unbelievably. For days I argued with this fellow before I could get him as I wanted him. But always I

triumphed . . . (he laughs) . . . and few people triumphed over Voltaire. And here . . . (he throws light switch on a peasant mother and child) . . . we have something that pleases me, though of no historic importance. It was done because I love to model children.

The group is a peasant mother, two children playing at her feet and a nursing babe at her breast.

9A. EXT. STREET IN FRONT OF MUSEUM
Worth, as he throws away cigarette impatiently and takes new place of concealment.

10. INT. MUSEUM
The three men are strolling toward the figure of Marie Antoinette.

GOLATILY:
   *But you have no right to hide such genius in a side street museum.[8]

IGOR (goes to light switch):
   You are too gracious. These things have some merit, I suspect . . . but this—(throws switch) . . . I am convinced, is fine. (Joining the group.)

GOLATILY (leaning close to figure):
   Even those delicate veins, the texture of this flesh—I have never seen anything more exquisite.

IGOR (laughing):
   My partner believes that I should build a horror chamber, immortalizing the hideous crimes and criminals of London. At such times Marie Antoinette has reassured me, she has promised me recognition for the devotion I gave to her.

GOLATILY:
   She will undoubtedly keep her promise.* If you'll

grant me the privilege, I'd like to submit this work to the Royal Academy when I get back.

IGOR (delighted):
You will have won the undying gratitude of us all. (Glancing over his shoulder.) Is that not so, Marie Antoinette?

GOLATILY (as they cross to door):
I regret I can't spend the time I'd like with your exhibition, but I'm going to worry the life out o' you when I come back. (The three laugh.)

IGOR:
It will always afford me great pleasure to see you. (They shake hands.)

GOLATILY:
Good night, sir.

IGOR:
Good night. (To Rasmussen.) And I am very grateful to you.

11.   EXT. MUSEUM   MAIN ENTRANCE
Door opens. Golatily and Rasmussen come through door. Igor is speaking.

IGOR:
Thank you so much for your visit and encouragement.

They bid each other good night cordially and the two stroll away, as Igor closes the door and pulls the blind.

12.   EXT. MUSEUM
The two men pass the spot where Worth has concealed himself. He peers after them from the shadows, then crosses street toward museum and walks toward door of entrance.

13.   INT. MUSEUM

Igor, with the exuberance of a delighted child, runs to the figure of Marie Antoinette and caresses her.

IGOR:

> You heard what he said. You heard this man who is very celebrated, what he said of you? (He backs away from the figure, laughing.) Ho-ho-ho, of course, you would say that. You always told me so, of course. (Then extending arms to include all the figures in the gallery.) *And you, my friends—Robespierre, Danton, Marat, Maximilian, Savonarola, all of you, how will you feel to be famous again?[9]

These figures, whom he has addressed individually in the last speech, are all on a raised platform or balcony, and he has turned and gestured toward each one as he named them. He now turns to Voltaire. Walking toward the figure and shaking his finger at it.

IGOR:

> And even you, who scoffed at immortality, who wrote so eloquently against the thought of immortality, you are experiencing it in spite of yourself.*

We hear the door open and Igor turns.

IGOR (surprised, questioningly):

> Hello! What are you doing here so late?

We hear footsteps of someone approaching him as the CAMERA SWINGS and Worth walks into picture.

WORTH (brusquely):

> I came back for some of the books. I am trying to straighten out the accounts. I don't hope to impress you, but I may as well tell you: We haven't a farthing!

IGOR (mildly, with no great concern):

> That is unfortunate.

14.   CLOSE-UP   WORTH
He is furious.

WORTH:
> You're right it's unfortunate! Fifteen thousand pounds it's cost me! And you say it's unfortunate, as though I'd spilled a spot of grog on my waistcoat.

CAMERA ANGLE WIDENS TO A

15.   CLOSE SHOT OF THE TWO

IGOR (returning to workbench, followed by Worth; Igor shrugs):
> Your money may have been well invested, my friend. Something important may come of all this.

WORTH:
> Something important has *got* to come of it! Do you know that the rent on this place isn't paid?

IGOR (sits at bench and starts to work):
> Is that a fact?

WORTH (angrily):
> No—I'm lying to amuse myself! (Leaning over bench confidentially.) Now look here, I've an idea that will get us out of all this. We haven't twopence between us, but we've got these. (Draws papers from pocket, slaps them on desk before Igor. Igor glances at them, then up at Worth in surprise.)

IGOR:
> Fire insurance!

WORTH:
> Yes, there's our way out. A fire in this place would give us ten thousand pounds.

Igor rises slowly, unable to believe what he hears.

IGOR:
> A fire! Is this your idea of humor, my friend?

58

WORTH (grimly):

> I want the money back I've thrown into this rubbish heap.

IGOR:

> You are asking to burn these people . . . you are asking? . . . (Growing excited, takes a few steps away from bench.)

16.   INT.MUSEUM   MED.SHOT

Igor makes a sweeping gesture that takes in the entire room.

IGOR:

> . . . to destroy all this?

WORTH:

> I'm not asking you anything. I'm *telling* you what I'm going to do!

IGOR:

> And you think I will permit this, my friend?

WORTH:

> You've *got* to permit it! Whose fault is it that no one comes here? The museum at Walston Lane does well enough, and why? They've got Jack the Ripper, Burke and Hare, the Mad Butcher, the Demon Barber of Fleet Street and things people pay to see.

IGOR:

> And they are welcome to them. To perpetuate such creatures is to celebrate their crimes.

WORTH:

> Well, what do you think I'm in this for? (Indicating figures, changing tone and attempting to cajole Igor.) Think of it, man, a match—a cigar stub—and ten thousand pounds to divide between us!

IGOR:

> You're insane.

WORTH:

> Not at all—let me show you how easily it can be done. (He strikes match and starts toward one of the figures.)

Igor springs and whirls him about. Worth strikes Igor viciously and they have a terrific struggle, in the course of which Worth seizes a spirit lamp used for warming wax and hurls it at Igor. He misses his mark, but the lighted lamp falls into the folds of the draperies of one of the figures standing next to that of Marie Antoinette. Igor screams his terror as he dashes to extinguish the flames, and Worth, springing on his back, overpowers him. By this time the fire is spreading to one of the other groups. Worth quickly snatches some of the flaming cloth from this group and tosses it at the feet of other figures. The figures are shown to be melting, gradually losing form, and finally the liquid wax itself ignites with a flash that is almost an explosion. Igor is seen to stir, and Worth, seizing a heavy staff from the hands of one of the figures, strikes him several times. Apparently satisfied that Igor is helpless, Worth now hurries to a rear door and makes his exit.[10]

17.   EXT. AREAWAY BACK OF MUSEUM

We see Worth come through door, panting and disheveled. He starts away and then returns and locks door, after which he runs from scene.

18.   INT. MUSEUM

Igor, dazed and weak, is struggling to his feet. He looks toward the figure of Marie Antoinette, its draperies now a mass of flame. He dashes toward it, catching it up in his arms, attempting to beat out the fire. The whole room now resembles the inside of a furnace, and as Igor, carrying the flaming figure, struggles toward the door, a portion of the ceiling collapses, barring his progress. He turns and staggers toward the rear. His clothes are blazing. He runs to a small iron trap in floor, near which is a group tableau of

Sidney Carton on the Guillotine. Lifting the cover, he discloses an empty drain barely large enough to permit the passage of his body. As he disappears through trap, the rope suspending the blade of the guillotine burns through and the knife falls, decapitating the figure, and the head rolls across the floor.[11]

FADE OUT

FADE IN ON

19.   SKYLINE OF NEW YORK (miniature)

On a building in the foreground is an electric sign, the full width of the building, which reads New York Express. There is a huge illuminated clock dial someplace beneath the sign. The clock shows one minute of twelve. As the picture fades in and the minute hand jumps abruptly to exactly twelve, another electric sign showing the numerals 1932[12] in red appears immediately beneath the sign New York Express. Simultaneous with this we hear the shrieks of sirens, the honking of automobile horns, the screech of boat whistles in the harbor, the ringing of bells, the rapid firing of a pistol somewhere in the distance, the shouting of the crowd, indicating the passing of the old year. These sounds, in varying degrees, continue all through the following scenes. As this shot dissolves, the tone dissolves with it to the single scream of a siren as we see

20.   STREET CORNER   A CROWD OF PEOPLE

An ambulance driving around the corner.

DISSOLVE TO:

21.   EXT. OF APARTMENT BUILDING

with all the windows lighted. Some windows still have Christmas ornaments in them. The CAMERA ON CRANE MOVES UP TO various windows. As the screaming of the siren and arrival of ambulance evidently attract the attention of the dwellers, several people open their windows and look out curiously. Some of them are holding cocktail glasses, and as the windows are opened we hear the

strains of radio music and other sounds of joyous cele-
brating. In the last window we see Igor in his legitimate
make-up—not as a horror person—looking at something
across the street.

CUT TO:

22.   EXT. OF OTHER APARTMENT HOUSE AT CORNER
The ambulance parked in front of it and a number of
curious people standing about. The door of the apartment
house is opened by a man in uniform, and we see a doctor
carrying a medical case coming out of the house. A newspaper reporter runs up the steps to meet him and says:

REPORTER:
    Anything new, Doc?

DOCTOR:
    Nothing we didn't tell you this afternoon. The
    coroner confirmed our opinion—it was suicide.

During this dialogue, two internes carrying a stretcher
descend the steps, pass the doctor and place stretcher in
ambulance, close door of ambulance, get on ambulance,
drive away, and again we hear the noise of the siren.

DISSOLVE TO:

INSERT: Of newspaper heading:
        THE NEW YORK EXPRESS
        WISHES ITS READERS
        A HAPPY NEW YEAR.
Single column article: ∙

            BEAUTIFUL JOAN GALE
                A SUICIDE
(*then in smaller type*)

            Show Girl Found Dead
              On Eve of New Year.
(*then the story*)
        While the Broadway she loved prepared
        to celebrate the New Year, Joan Gale,

62

beautiful show girl, lay dead by her own hand, it was discovered late yesterday afternoon. A maid at the Denton Hotel, where the butterfly girl occupied an expensive suite, entered her apartment at noon and found her clad in pajamas, etc., etc.

(*single column picture of Joan Gale*)

All through reading paper we hear New York celebration noises.

DISSOLVE TO:

23. NARROW DOWNTOWN STREET (probably West Broadway)　　　　　　　　　　　　　　　　　NIGHT
with elevated road extending full width of street. An old-fashioned, disreputable brick building, with an iron grating along the edge of walk, beyond which is an areaway and a flight of stone steps, leading to basement door. There is also a door on the street level. The figure of a man approaches the house. The CAMERA SEES only his back. We hear the distant sound of the New York celebration, and two girls, passing the man who is walking AWAY FROM CAMERA, blow horns at him and throw confetti on him. He does not answer. He passes them and admits himself to house with latchkey.

24. INT. WORTH HOUSE
CAMERA FOLLOWS him through a corridor into a room as dilapidated and forbidding as the exterior of the house. The room, evidently used as an office, is furnished with an ancient, battered desk and chairs. The walls are bare, and in places the paper, and even bits of plaster, have been torn away.

The figure of the man enters and throws on the lights. He goes to the desk, picks up a phone and dials a number, sitting in swivel chair with his back to CAMERA. He gets his number.

MAN:
> Hello, is that you, Tim? . . . Tim, I'm sorry but I've got to have that tonight . . . I've *got* to have it.

CAMERA TRAVELS TOWARD him as he slowly turns to face it.

MAN:
> No, I need it right away.

By this time we get a

25.   CLOSE-UP OF WORTH'S FACE
and we see that it is the man who burned the museum. All through the phone conversation we hear the muffled shouts, the horns, etc. of the New Year celebration.

MAN:
> Who's on at the gate? . . . you say Joe? . . . Well, then you can get it out all right. I'll have the truck right down there. The harness bull down there is oke. I fixed that this afternoon.
>
> DISSOLVE TO:

26.   STREET OUTSIDE THE MORGUE
A policeman walking leisurely along his beat reaches the iron gate and glances up at the sign above the arch, which reads Morgue. We hear the distant shouting, singing, trumpeting. After the officer has disappeared, an upper window of the building opens and the hideous face of the Monster appears as he leans out of the window following the progress of the policeman along the street.

27.   INT. MORGUE   FULL SHOT
(It is necessary to give this business in detail, but it will be played quickly as the Monster moves with astonishing rapidity.)
The room is almost in darkness, the only light coming from a window well upstage and at one side. We see dimly a row of slabs mounted on wheels. They are all occupied, the bodies being covered with sheets. The Monster glides quickly among them with a flashlight, turning down the

sheets and inspecting the faces, finally locating the one he seems to have been in search of. CAMERA COMES TO A

28.   CLOSE SHOT OF MONSTER
bending over slab as he examines figure illuminated by flashlight. We do not see the features of the corpse.[13] As the Monster straightens up, he utters a horrible gurgling, retching murmur of joy, and we see him clearly for the first time.

29.   CLOSE-UP   MONSTER
A black-cloaked figure, disproportionate and grotesque, the face a horrible formless mass of scarred tissue. He has practically no forehead. His face is a shriveled bald pate of seared skin and bone, which recedes to a pointed cranium of unnatural contour. His eyes are alight with fanaticism and insanity. The face is a blot of drawn, unwholesomely colored, hairless skin. He is lipless, noseless, and what traces of human features remain are frightfully distorted. CAMERA RECEDES TO

30.   MED. SHOT
and TRAVELS WITH him as he pushes the carriage quickly to the back window and places it against the sill, feet first.

31.   CLOSE SHOT AT WINDOW
He opens the window, which has a single bar from top to bottom dividing its center. He leans out and whistles. During all of this we have been hearing the joyous shouts of the merrymakers. In answer to his signal there is a single whistle from someplace below. He throws the sheet aside and fastens a rope around and under the arms of the corpse, which he pushes slowly across the sill into space. After lowering the body, there is a whistle from below. He throws the remainder of the coil of rope out the window, but on the opposite side of the upright bar, so that the rope forms a double strand outside, permitting him to slide to ground level. CAMERA ANGLE WIDENS and we PAN

WITH the Monster as he returns the slab to its original position. He hears someone approaching and stretches out at length on the slab, covering himself with the sheet. The voices grow louder and the CAMERA SWINGS, PICKING UP two attendants and FOLLOWING them as they enter. One of them throws on the lights, and they wheel another body into place beside the slab on which the Monster is concealed.

FIRST ATTENDANT:
New Year's Eve ain't what it used to be. This is only the second one tonight.

SECOND ATTENDANT:
Yeah, times are sure tough.

FIRST ATTENDANT:
What happened to this one?

SECOND ATTENDANT:
Husband slapped her full of lumps . . . said she talked too much.

The men turn and start out of the scene. The body, having just been embalmed, has a muscular reflex and rises to a rigid semisitting posture.[14]

FIRST ATTENDANT (frightened):
What's that?

SECOND ATTENDANT:
Embalming fluid makes 'em jump.

He returns coolly and pushes the body into its proper position. The action causes a horrible rasping sound, peculiar to corpses.

SECOND ATTENDANT (coldly):
Ain't that just like a woman . . . always has to have the last word.

CAMERA FOLLOWS the two men as they exit in the direction from which they came, throwing off the lights and shutting the door after them. CAMERA PANS BACK to the Monster as he springs from the slab, and FOLLOWS him as he crosses to the window, climbs through and lowers himself over the sill.[15]

INSERT: Showing base of upright bar of window with rope looped over. Evidently safe on the ground, the Monster pulls one end of rope, and we see it running around bar until the end disappears.

During this insert, we hear a crescendo of horns, shouts, etc., finally dominated by the clack of a wooden noisemaker, that blends gradually with the myriad clicking of a number of typewriters, as we

DISSOLVE TO:

32.   CLOSE-UP OF TYPEWRITER AND HANDS OPERATING MACHINE
CAMERA PULLS BACK:

33.   COMPOSING ROOM OF THE NEW YORK EXPRESS   NIGHT
CAMERA PICKS UP a door at the end of a line of tables, with typewriters, where rewrite men are busy on copy, copy boys bringing them assignments, carrying away completed stories, etc. Sign on door reads Managing Editor. CAMERA SWINGS the length of the lane, PICKS UP door at opposite end of room, and with a sudden, terrific blast of steam whistles, etc., the door opens and the girl, Florence (Glenda Farrell), appears through door, obviously squiffy, leading a nondescript mongrel dog.[16] She carries a long, cheap tin horn. The man nearest the door glances up from his work.

FLORENCE:
   Gentlemen of the Daily Grind: 1932 salutes you with a fanfare of golden brass! (Takes hand from behind her and blows on rubber "Bronx cheer" rattler.)

The men laugh. Florence produces a bottle of Scotch.

FIRST MAN (pointing significantly toward managing editor's door):
   Save your breath. Hard-Tack wants to see you.

FLORENCE:
> I don't want to see him—he hurts my eyes.

FIRST MAN:
> No kiddin', he's sore as a dog.

FLORENCE (to dog):
> Move over Kelly. I'm in the dog house!

MAN (laughs):
> Where'd you get the stag hound?

FLORENCE:
> He's not a stag hound. His name is Kelly and he's a police dog.

MAN (patting the pup; others gather around also stroking him):
> What do you mean police dog?

FLORENCE:
> Plain-clothes man. (Addressing room.) Come on, slaves, drink and be merry for tomorrow you might be appointed correspondent to Washington . . . a fate worse than death.

MAN:
> Listen, Flo, cut it out. Hard-Tack is pretty sore.

FLORENCE (laughs):
> Ain't that something. The mad monk of Manhattan. Here goes nothing. (Crosses to door lettered Managing Editor and, as she exits through it, shouts over shoulder.) Listen to the animal cracker roar like a lion![17]

34.   INT. EDITOR'S OFFICE
The managing editor (Frank McHugh), a man of about thirty-five, not physically unattractive, but rather grim, is seated at his desk—an intense worker, plainly impatient with anyone who loafs on the job.[18]

(In the following scene we establish that, while he quarrels continually throughout the picture with the girl, there is an underlying and very strong bond of friendship and respect between the two.)

The door opens and, as Florence appears, we hear the last few words of her preceding speech. She closes the door, leaning against it.

FLORENCE:

As *I* live and breathe and wear spats . . . the prince.

EDITOR (looking up angrily):

Been doing experiments with Scotch and soda again?

FLORENCE (disheveled and obviously with an "edge"):

Where did you get the news item? (Sarcastically.) From a little bird?

EDITOR:

Yeah. (Discards sheaf of papers and looks up.) Have a pleasant vacation?

FLORENCE:

Charming. More delightful people crippled.

EDITOR:

Great. Consider yourself crippled—financially. See if you can jar your charming friends loose from enough to eat on.

FLORENCE:

Meaning what?

EDITOR:

That you're a sure bet to place in the bread line. There's no room on this rag for the purely ornamental. You're easy on the eyes and pretty conceited about it.

He returns to his work. CAMERA FOLLOWS Florence and comes to a

69

35. CLOSE SHOT OF FLORENCE

as she walks down and puts her arm over editor's shoulder.

FLORENCE:

Is mama's dumpling getting tough?

He pushes her away from him.

EDITOR:

I'm through clowning. You're all washed up. Get out!

FLORENCE (straightening up):

What do you mean, you poor ham! This is New Year's!

EDITOR:

All right, what about it? We get out a paper just the same. Did you ever stop to think of that?

FLORENCE:

Well, is it my fault if nothing happens?

He rises and, taking Florence angrily by the arm, almost drags her to the window. He points to the street below. There is an alternating red and green light through the window, as though it came from an electric sign across the street.

EDITOR:

Look down there! Nothing happening! Out of that insane mob you say there's nothing happening? There's a story in every person down there.

Florence giggles.

FLORENCE (with elaborate sarcasm):

And how does one go about getting these human documents, may I inquire?

EDITOR (caustically):

That is none of our business. (Pushing her suddenly so that she stumbles to door.) But you bring me

70

something for the next edition if it's only a recipe for spaghetti! (Turns quickly and sneers at her.)

FLORENCE (turning to door, shouts):
Quick, Watson, the cookbook!

She exits and slams door. He looks after her angrily, as he returns to his desk.

36.   INT. COMPOSING ROOM   FULL SHOT
as Florence reenters. Sits on desk of last man she spoke to.

FLORENCE:
What a sense of humor that guy has. Thinks a hangover is a Jewish holiday. I'm fired!

MAN:
I told you he was a sore.

FLORENCE:
Stories scarcer than caviar at a street cleaner's banquet, and he says, bring me a yarn. All I have to do is get a story.

MAN:
Here's a wow.

He whispers to her. She straightens up and looks at him contemptuously. She crosses to door. Turning back, she sees the mongrel she brought in and calls.

FLORENCE:
Hey, come here, Kelly. I don't want you hanging around with that guy. He's been reading naughty stories.

She and the dog exit.[19]

DISSOLVE TO:

INSERT: CLOSE-UP OF COVER OF MAGAZINE
entitled "Naughty Stories." Shows scantily attired figure of a girl dancer.

CAMERA DRAWS BACK TO

71

37.   CLOSE-UP OF DESK SERGEANT ABSORBED IN MAGAZINE
at 47th Street Police Station.

38.   FULL SHOT   POLICE STATION RECEPTION ROOM
Several uniformed men seated, reading late editions, etc.
Florence enters with gay, almost rowdy camaraderie and
thumps one of the officers on the back.

FLORENCE:
Happy New Year, Ambrose!

He straightens and looks up.

OFFICER:
Hello, Mrs. Dempsey. I don't see how they're ever
going to settle that heavyweight argument while
you're around. (Rubbing shoulder.)

39.   CLOSE SHOT   DESK
Florence crosses to desk and, reaching over, pulls the
magazine out of the sergeant's hand.

FLORENCE:
Happy New Year, sweetheart. How's your sex life?
(Glances at magazine.) Oh-oh! (Hands it back to
him.)

SERGEANT (shouts):
Call the Homicide Squad!

FLORENCE:
How's every little thing?

SERGEANT:
Fine. You're the first reporter in here for two hours.
You people seeing the old year out?

FLORENCE:
I'm people which the old year saw out. I'm canned,
fired!

SERGEANT:
No kiddin'.

FLORENCE:

I've got to make news, if I have to bite a dog. (Looks around suddenly.) Hey, Kelly! Oh, mi gosh, even *he* walked out on me.

SERGEANT:

I've got a story for you. You know the Joan Gale girl?

FLORENCE (unenthusiastically):

Yes, she committed suicide yesterday. That's not news. I heard about it last year.

SERGEANT (mimicking her):

Oh, yeah? Maybe she *didn't* commit suicide. She *may* have been murdered!

FLORENCE (startled):

No foolin'—any suspect?

SERGEANT:

Do you know George Winton?

FLORENCE:

Old Howard Winton's cub?

SERGEANT:

That's the one.

FLORENCE (aghast):

They don't suspect *him*?

SERGEANT:

Don't they? He's down at The Tombs right now.

FLORENCE (threateningly):

Say, if you're stringin' me, Old-Timer . . .

SERGEANT (snaps):

Why would I string y'? They were sweeties until a month ago.

FLORENCE:

What does that prove?

SERGEANT:
> Nothing. Only she may have tried to blackmail him. You know such things have happened. Anyway, he was at her apartment a few hours before she was found dead.

FLORENCE (enthusiastically):
> Hotcha! Saved, one job!

She reaches for the telephone on the sergeant's desk. He snatches it away from her.

SERGEANT:
> Press room for yours.

40. FULL SHOT   POLICE STATION RECEPTION ROOM
as Florence starts to door.

SERGEANT:
> But hold everything. Let me give you the rest of the dirt.

She turns in door.

FLORENCE:
> Make it snappy, Colonel.

SERGEANT:
> There's an autopsy ordered at Bellevue immediately. You better skip over there.

FLORENCE (starting through door):
> Don't give this to anybody else, will you?

SERGEANT:
> It's all yours.

FLORENCE:
> Thanks.

As she exits, she throws switch, leaving the entire room in darkness. There is a shout of protest from the men, which blends with the sound of an elevated train as we

DISSOLVE TO:

41. EXT. WORTH HOUSE
A small covered truck drives up and stops. A man riding beside the driver jumps down and, glancing quickly up and down the street, runs down the basement steps and rings bell.

42. CLOSE SHOT   BASEMENT DOOR
Lattice is drawn aside and a man peers out.

DOOR TENDER:
   Get it all right?

DRIVER'S COMPANION:
   Yes . . . let's get it off the truck. Lend us a hand.

The door opens.

DOOR TENDER (calling over his shoulder):
   Hey, Sparrow—come on!

Another figure appears, a furtive little man who occasionally, throughout the picture, rubs hand across nose as cocaine fiends are known to do.[20] He seems to be in a very nervous state. Together, the four men remove a large oblong case from the truck and carry it downstairs into the basement.

43. INT. A LARGE, SPARSELY FURNISHED BASEMENT ROOM
There are a number of crates and boxes piled in one corner, and on a plain kitchen table, center, there are a number of bottles, glasses, etc. The four men enter and deposit the case, which is marked Fragile—Handle with Care, on the floor.

DOOR TENDER:
   How about a little shot?

As the men approach the table, CAMERA MOVES UP and we get a CLOSE-UP, separately, of each of the four men as they drink. They are all of the urban criminal type. As CAMERA PULLS BACK, the truck driver and his companion start toward door.

TRUCK DRIVER:
> Happy New Year!

DRIVER'S COMPANION:
> See you some more!

The two exit.

44.   FULL SHOT OF BASEMENT ROOM
as the two men exit. Door tender turns toward Sparrow
and CAMERA MOVES UP TO A

45.   CLOSE SHOT OF THE TWO

DOOR TENDER:
> No use of your hangin' around here. He told me not
> to give you anything tonight.

SPARROW (obviously in highly nervous state):
> Where is he? Call him down, willya? I've got to talk to
> him.

A door upstage opens. The two turn and CAMERA PULLS
BACK as Worth enters.

WORTH (to Sparrow):
> I thought I told you to stay out of here!

Sparrow crosses eagerly toward Worth.

SPARROW:
> Hello, Joe. I wouldn't bother you, but I'm all in. My
> nerves are all shot.

WORTH (contemptuously):
> Your nerves are not all that are going to be shot, you
> sneaky rat—you've been talking again!

Worth hits Sparrow and knocks him down.

WORTH (to door tender):
> Give him a deck.

CAMERA PULLS BACK TO

46. FULL SHOT OF BASEMENT ROOM
as door tender extracts a small parcel from drawer in table and tosses it to Sparrow, who grabs it eagerly and struggles to his feet.

WORTH (threateningly):
And understand this, you get nothing more from me until you show me something! And the next time you speak out of turn, you're going to have bad luck.

As Worth finishes speech, he slaps Sparrow's face.

SPARROW (conscious only of the package given him):
Thanks . . . thanks.

FADE OUT

FADE IN   NIGHT
47. TOP OF TABLE   PITCHER OF ICE WATER, GLASSES
Florence approaches table, pours a glass of ice water and, before drinking it, presses it to her forehead and temple. CAMERA SWINGS showing rest of room, which is evidently a morgue surgery. There are several officials, internes, a nurse, two doctors, two or three plain-clothes men and a policeman in uniform who is standing guard at the door. One of the plain-clothes men, who evidently knows Florence, crosses and speaks to her.

DETECTIVE:
Feelin' tough?

FLORENCE:
I've got a case of jitters that will cop the Pulitzer prize. If they drag this out too long, they'll have another corpse on their hands.

CAMERA SWINGS TO:

48.   CLOSE SHOT OF TWO DOCTORS

FIRST DOCTOR:
When I was called, doctor, the girl had been dead for possibly three or four hours. My examination showed clearly that she died of laudanum poisoning.[21] I thought at first it might have been an accident, an overdose. Her eyes indicated that she used narcotics frequently.

SECOND DOCTOR:
What was the police theory?

FIRST DOCTOR:
Suicide.

SECOND DOCTOR:
Leave any message?

FIRST DOCTOR:
No. That's why I thought death might have been accidental.

One of the plain-clothes men joins the two doctors.

FIRST DOCTOR:
Who got the information about Winton, Flannery?

DETECTIVE:
Everyone knows they was livin' together. *But the way they fought you'd of thought they was married.[22]

FIRST DOCTOR:
Been separated quite some time, hadn't they?

DETECTIVE:
Yeah.* He was playin' up to some other twist. Winton's in bad because he left there just before she folded up.

SECOND DOCTOR:
>Well, if she committed suicide, with laudanum, she probably took it in its crude form, and we'll find it in that or very close to that state. If someone gave it to her, it would be diluted.

DETECTIVE:
>How could he give it to her?

FIRST DOCTOR:
>In a cup of coffee or a glass of whiskey.

The door bursts open and one of the attendants rushes in and, going directly to the two doctors, speaks.

ATTENDANT:
>The Gale body is gone!

FIRST DOCTOR:
>Gone? What are you talking about?

SECOND DOCTOR (speaking almost simultaneous with the first):
>The body gone! Absurd!

DETECTIVE:
>Wait a minute. (To the attendant.) What happened? What do you mean the body's gone?

ATTENDANT:
>Just that. It's gone—vanished—disappeared!

DETECTIVE:
>You mean somebody stole the body!

FLORENCE:
>No. It got up and walked down to the cemetery to dig up a date.

Detectives give Florence a dirty glance.

ATTENDANT (excitedly):
>We went for the body and found the slab empty and the window to the alley open.

FLORENCE:
Hot dog, death on a holiday![23]

DETECTIVE (calling to other plain-clothes man):
Come on, Flannery!

They leave the room hurriedly, followed by the attendant. Florence, her hand to her head, sways.

FLORENCE:
Boy, oh boy! And he asked for a story. Is his face red!

She looks around, sees phone, grabs it up and calls for a number.

FLORENCE:
Bryant two six two six.

She waits a moment and then jiggles the receiver impatiently.

FLORENCE (shouting):
Operator! (Operator answers. Florence, sarcastically.) My, my, how you have grown. (Quickly.) Will you get that number, Mrs. Van Winkle![24]

49.   EDITOR'S OFFICE
The phone on his desk is ringing. He picks it up.

EDITOR (barks):
Hello!

50.   CLOSE-UP   FLORENCE IN PHONE BOOTH

FLORENCE (into phone):
Hello, Slug . . . kill that Winton story for this! Joan Gale's body, not John Brown's . . . Joan Gale's body was snatched from the morgue two minutes ago! I'm here now! Yeah, there were nine or ten witnesses! Nope, they didn't talk! They're pretty stiff. No, dope, not drunk, they're dead!

80

51.   EDITOR'S DESK   CLOSE SHOT   EDITOR INTO PHONE

EDITOR:

> Can the clowning! Great! Great! Tear down to The
> Tombs and get to Winton! I'll have Harry write the
> first flash! (Something she says evidently angers him
> to the point that he holds the telephone away from
> him. Half angry, as though *it* were responsible, he
> barks.) A cow does that . . . and gives milk besides.
> (He slams up receiver.)

DISSOLVE TO:

52.   CLOSE-UP   PRINTING PRESSES IN LARGE NEWSPAPER PLANT

The papers being pushed out on rack as they are delivered
from press. CAMERA PULLS BACK as foreman picks up a
copy to examine it for type.

INSERT: CLOSE-UP OF NEWSPAPER

showing scare headline describing arrest of George Winton who is held in jail and an autopsy ordered. On front
page is a photograph of Winton. CAMERA HOLDS for a
moment on photograph, which

DISSOLVES TO:

53.   CLOSE SHOT OF WINTON BEHIND BARS

54.   INT. CELL IN THE TOMBS

Winton seated on the edge of his cot. CAMERA SWINGS
AROUND to reveal the cell door being opened by a guard.
Florence enters and goes to boy. He is a rather handsome,
but weak, dissipated type, who arouses our sympathy
without winning our respect.

FLORENCE:

> How do you do. I'm from the Express.

Winton looks up. When he speaks, his sentences are
halting and broken. He's badly frightened.

WINTON:

> Yeah. I suppose you people will crucify me for
> something I didn't do. (His voice rising almost to

falsetto.) I didn't! You understand that? . . . I didn't
do it! She—tried before—(Buries his face in hands,
choking sob.)

FLORENCE (sits on cot beside him, pats his shoulder):
Come on, old man, that won't do. You know you're
innocent until proven guilty.

WINTON (springing to feet and pacing back and forth):
Yes, sure, that's fine. While I'm proving my inno-
cence, you people are going to uncover every petty
kid trick I ever did . . . you're going to write editorials
about every cocktail I ever drank. Anything that any
sane, normal person might have done will have a
sinister meaning, if I did it. (He is almost crying at
this point, sinking on cot.) Go on! Get out! I don't
want to talk to you! (He rises and crosses quickly as
though to open door, then, realizing that he is locked
in, leans, face against the bars, fighting to control
tears.)

Florence follows him and places her hand on his shoulder.

FLORENCE:
Listen, kid. You're in a tough spot, and you can make
it a whole lot easier for yourself if you cut out the
cry-baby stuff—

WINTON (whirling, faces her):
Cry-baby!

FLORENCE:
That's what I said.

WINTON (angrily):
My lawyers will be on the job in a little while, and I
warn you people anything you print about me you've
got to prove. Dad won't stand for—

FLORENCE:
Your dad has stood for plenty. Now let's get down to
cases. When did you see the Gale girl last?

WINTON:

For a few minutes the afternoon before—before—

FLORENCE:

Hmmm. Why didn't you tell that to the police?

WINTON (hysterically):

They didn't give me a chance. We had a couple of drinks and she was all right then. She seemed happy.

FLORENCE:

Uh-huh. Do you remember what she said? What did you talk about?

WINTON:

She laughed and told me that we were being silly, that we didn't care for each other any more but we needn't hate each other . . . (He sobs through the finish of this speech.) . . . She said she wanted to be friends.

FLORENCE:

I see. Was that all she said?

WINTON (recovering self-control to some degree):

We planned a trip for her. I was going to send her to Bermuda.

FLORENCE:

You weren't going with her?

WINTON:

No. (Paces floor, pounding palm of hand with fist desperately.) Why didn't I take her out somewhere? But she was laughing and seemed so happy.

FLORENCE:

Well, let's get back to the case in hand. They ordered an autopsy and discovered her body had been stolen from the morgue.

WINTON (his nerves quite shattered):

Stolen! What are you trying to do to me? . . . You're

working with the police! . . . You're trying to make me say something that can be used against me! You're trying . . .

FLORENCE:

Hold on, hold on. I'm trying to *help* you, if you're on the square, and I think you are.

WINTON:

Then why are you telling me a crazy lie? . . .

FLORENCE:

That happens to be the truth.

WINTON:

Who'd steal her body?

FLORENCE:

That's what they're going to ask *you.*

Winton seems stunned. Guard appears in door.

GUARD:

Time's up.

FLORENCE:

Be right with you. (Turning, pats Winton on shoulder.) Keep a stiff upper lip, kid. I think you'll come out okay.

The guard opens the door and as she exits, we

DISSOLVE TO:

55. CLOSE SHOT OF EDITOR AT HIS DESK
He is leaning back in swivel chair, listening attentively. We hear Florence's voice, but do not see her.

FLORENCE'S VOICE:

The whole thing sounded on the up and up to me. The poor kid is too scared to lie. He's getting a raw deal.

CAMERA PULLS BACK to include Florence, seated in chair close to editor's desk.

EDITOR (sarcastically):
> Well ain't that a shame. Nice little chappie that wouldn't harm a fly . . . everybody picking on the little fellow.

FLORENCE:
> If this kid was some unknown soda jerker, they wouldn't have pinched him. But he's George Winton and they're playing him up. It's a Roman holiday for every paper hat editor in New York.

EDITOR (glancing from desk where he has been idly scratching with a pencil):
> Why the goose pimples? If he wasn't social register—if it was somebody like me, you'd be trying to *hang* him.

FLORENCE:
> I wouldn't be trying, beloved. I *would* hang him! And another thing, all this gaga about the body disappearing. Eight bodies have been stolen in New York within the last eighteen months. Doesn't it seem more reasonable to hook this up from that angle?

EDITOR (laughs):
> And ruin a perfectly good story? Don't be silly.

FLORENCE:
> No, I mean it. I think this kid's entitled to a break.

EDITOR:
> He's getting a break, ain't he? He's front page.

FLORENCE:
> You give me a pain!

EDITOR:
> I'm glad to hear it. When did you go in for crusading in the cause of justice? This lousy mug, with all the money in the world, has had two or three nasty affairs. He's kept out o' print because his great-grandfather was smarter than the Indians.

FLORENCE:

Well, anyway, he couldn't have copped that body—he was in jail.

EDITOR:

You don't think he'd be sap enough to do the job himself. I hope they give him the works. Even if he didn't kill the kid, he's responsible for her death, and they can fry him any time without making me sore.

FLORENCE (rising angrily):

Well, I won't work on it from that angle.

EDITOR:

Oh, you won't—you were pretty tough about Judge Ramsey—a little while ago—

FLORENCE:

And they never proved anything against him.

EDITOR:

Except that he disappeared when things got too hot.

FLORENCE:

Or was bumped off by someone who was afraid of him.

EDITOR:

Whooey—he took a run-out powder.

FLORENCE:

Well, that's got nothing to do with this case. Can I handle this my way?

EDITOR:

You cannot. I'm still editor of this sheet.

FLORENCE:

All right, you said I was fired. Well, I quit! Give the assignment to somebody else. (Starts toward door.)

EDITOR (laughs):

Hey, come here, Sob-sister!

FLORENCE:

Nope, I'm through!

Her hand is on the knob. CAMERA FOLLOWS editor who rises and, following, embraces her roughly and pats her on shoulder as he releases her.

EDITOR:

Go ahead, screwy! Do it your own way.

As he returns to desk, she takes a step after him.

FLORENCE:

On the square, Jimmy, if you'd seen Winton down there—I'm not holding a brief for him—maybe he's a dirty pup, but he's scared and hysterical—and so kinda dumb and worthless . . .

EDITOR:

Great! . . . If he's worthless we'll give him away as a bridge prize. Come on—beat it. It's five o'clock. You need some sleep.

FLORENCE (going through door):

No, there's another point I want to iron out.

EDITOR:

Sleep on it . . . we'll get it tomorrow.

Holds picture that he drew away from him, looking at it critically. Florence moves back of him to glance at it. He hands it to her.

EDITOR:

Your portrait.

INSERT: OF PICTURE

which is a crude sketch of Mickey Mouse on horseback, charging a windmill with a long lance.

FLORENCE:

Which one is me? The horse?

EDITOR (throws tobacco pouch at her):
Get out of here.

Florence dodges it, and exits laughing.

FADE OUT

FADE IN   DAY

56.   CLOSE-UP OF THREE CITY STREET-SWEEPERS' PUSH BROOMS
held end to end, pushing ahead of them a large quantity of
confetti, bits of paper and refuse of the hilarious night
before. CAMERA PULLS BACK, revealing three street-
sweepers. In the background we see the sign:

LONDON WAX MUSEUM—GRAND OPENING
TONIGHT
FIRST TIME IN AMERICA

and in front of the place, as CAMERA MOVES UP AGAIN TO
the entrance, we see a janitor sweeping off the sidewalk.
He is a strange, unwholesome-looking character. He has
swept most of the sidewalk, pushing the collected debris
into a pile in the gutter, when his attention is caught by
the protruding end of a whiskey bottle which shows in
the pile. He picks up the bottle and sees that there is a little
bit of liquid left in it, and he drains it, drop by drop, into
his mouth. He stoops to examine the pile further.

IGOR'S VOICE (off scene):
Otto! Otto! Get in here![25]

CAMERA FOLLOWS him as he turns and goes into the
museum.

57.   INT. MUSEUM   MED. SHOT OF IGOR
In background we see a veritable beehive of activity. A
number of workmen, including painters, carpenters, are
busy building and designing screenlike backgrounds for
the various exhibits, placing figures on platforms, etc. In
the center of the room, watching them, is Ivan Igor. CAM-
ERA MOVES TO A

88

58.   CLOSE SHOT OF IGOR

He is much changed, but still recognizable as the man we knew before the fire. His beard and hair are almost white and have been permitted to grow to far greater length, but the features are essentially the same, except that when he speaks or moves his face is strangely immobile. He is seated in a wheelchair, which is propelled by sprocket wheels on the arms of the chair. In order to manage this, there is a special cup or basket attached to the handles, as his hands are hideously deformed and practically useless for the purpose. He is impatient and angry with the workers, venting his anger immediately the janitor appears. Igor propels the chair forward.

59.   MED. SHOT   IGOR AND JANITOR

Igor, stopping, points angrily at floor immediately surrounding some of the groups, where shavings, excelsior and other packing material and debris are scattered.

IGOR (to janitor):
> Does it take you all morning to sweep that patch of sidewalk? Come, clean up this mess, and don't try to sweep this trash behind those screens. I want it removed.

JANITOR:
> Yes, sir.

Starts to clean up around nearest group. Igor wheels toward another group, FOLLOWED BY CAMERA, and addresses workmen angrily.

IGOR:
> Come, look, you fellows. You spend two days on something that should have taken two hours.

One of the workmen turns angrily.

WORKMAN:
> Say, listen, *Old-Timer*, they abolished slavery in this country a long time ago.

IGOR:

> Is it slavery to do what you're being paid for? I have announced the opening of this museum tonight.

Wheels angrily away. The workman laughs.[26] CAMERA FOLLOWS Igor as he wheels to end of museum where Hugo and Ralph are at work putting the finishing touches on two individual figures. Hugo is a man of middle age, with an insane, crafty face, unkempt hair and several days' growth of beard. He smiles continually to himself as though some secret of his own amused him. He is deaf and dumb and when excited or angry emits strange terrifying growls similar to the noises we heard the Monster utter. Ralph is rather a nice-looking youngster and seems engrossed in what he is doing.

60.   CLOSE SHOT

Igor comes to a stop near Ralph and sits inspecting his work.

IGOR (bitingly):

> If my curiosity is not too great, would you mind telling me what manner of animal this is you are designing?

RALPH:

> One of the maids-in-waiting for that Elizabethan group.[27]

IGOR (raising his hands to heaven):

> And he isn't struck dead! This man, he lives! It would be interesting to know, young man, where and when you studied anatomy.

RALPH (steps back a little and looks critically at the figure):

> That doesn't seem so bad to me. What is wrong with it?

Mystery of the Wax Museum

IGOR:

Everything, my friend. And you hope to be a great
sculptor—(Laugh.) A great sculptor. Look—this
forearm is at least two inches too long.

RALPH:

But the composition as a whole—I've tried to keep a
sketchy freedom.

IGOR:

If it is freedom to represent people with limbs that
don't match—cripples—you have achieved your
purpose. Anatomy! Heaven forgive you. You must
have studied with a sideshow of freaks!

CAMERA SWINGS as Igor whirls chair and sees Hugo's
piece.

IGOR:

And this fellow! Look, I ask you . . . look what this
cobbler is doing!

Ralph grins. Igor takes one of the crutches that ride beside
him on chair and, reaching out, pokes Hugo's shoulder.
Hugo turns with a startled growl.

IGOR (pointing with crutch to figure which looks not un-
like Hugo himself—shouts):

What is this? Are you so beautiful that you make
everything in your own likeness?[28]

Hugo utters an uncanny sound identified with deaf-
mutes. Igor, realizing that Hugo doesn't hear him, just
waves him back to work.

IGOR:

It's a great mercy of Providence that this fellow cannot
hear. (Turning back to Ralph, suddenly extends two
horribly maimed, clawlike hands toward Ralph.)
Look! Look at those claws! If I had those hands of

yours, I would show you the meaning of what you are trying to do. All those beautiful things that were destroyed I could restore. It is a great irony that you people without souls should have hands.

61.   EXT. ALLEY ENTRANCE   REAR OF MUSEUM
We see a truck backing in, and Sparrow, whom we first saw at Worth's house, climbs down from the driver's seat and enters museum.

62.   INT. MUSEUM
Igor is still speaking.

IGOR:
But go on, go back to work. It is hopeless to talk to such people.

He suddenly stops and turns his head. CAMERA SWINGS TO FOLLOW his line of vision and PICKS UP rear entrance as door opens and Sparrow enters. Igor wheels chair rapidly toward Sparrow, CAMERA FOLLOWING.

IGOR (eagerly):
Have you got it? Is it completed?

SPARROW:
Yes, sir, it's here on the truck, but it's pretty heavy— I'll need help.

IGOR (turns and shouts):
Otto! You and one of those other fellows! Come help Professor Darcey.[29]

Janitor comes forward, followed by two workmen.

JANITOR:
Yes, sir.

IGOR:
And hurry, please. This figure has still to be mounted and dressed.

Sparrow exits with three men, leaving door open. Igor wheels back toward Ralph and Hugo. He laughs delightedly, addressing Ralph.

IGOR:

> And now, my friend, you are to see something that one can in truth describe as art. Professor Darcey doesn't try to keep freedom and sketchiness in his figures. He is an artist. He works at home, hours, when such people as you are loafing. He is an artist.

The four men carry in a long, narrow box similar to the one that was delivered to Worth.

SPARROW:

> Shall we unpack it?

IGOR:

> Yes.

One of the workmen takes a claw hammer from strap in overalls and starts removing the lid as Igor wheels himself quickly toward Sparrow and the workers. CAMERA FOLLOWS and, as the lid of the box is removed, some burlap and other packing materials lifted out, and the box raised on end, we see the head, shoulders and one arm of a beautiful, lifelike figure of a girl. We identify the face immediately as that of Joan Gale. As the workers go about removing the rest of the packing, Igor whirls and addresses the other workers who have advanced and stand admiring the figure.

IGOR:

> Get back to work! You will have plenty of time to look at this.

As the workers return to their various jobs, one of them grins.

WORKER:

> Some mama![30]

(Note: The museum is, in all essentials, identical with the institution in London, the one figure missing from the restored ensemble being that of Marie Antoinette.)

63. CLOSE SHOT OF IGOR AND SPARROW
close to wall on which hangs a photo of Igor as a young man standing beside statue of Marie Antoinette.

IGOR:
It is exquisite—almost as beautiful as the original. (Points to picture on wall.) I hope one day to have you restore Marie Antoinette. (Sparrow is in a highly nervous state, which Igor detects.)

SPARROW:
I'd be glad to, Mr. Igor. (Leaning close to Igor—in subdued tone.) I think I'll have somethin' to tell you soon.

IGOR:
You have done well, and now I, too, have something for you. Come.

64. TELEPHONE BOOTH NEAR ENTRANCE OF MUSEUM
Ralph approaches and enters it. We see him dial for a number.

65. CLOSE SHOT OF WALL PHONE
which rings and Charlotte Duncan (Fay Wray) enters scene and answers it.[31] We see that in stature and face she is almost identical with the lost figure of Marie Antoinette.

CHARLOTTE (into phone):
Hello. (Laughs.) Oh, hello, dear. I was just thinking of you. . . . I was, too . . . no, I haven't forgotten.
CUT TO:

94

66.   RALPH AT PHONE

RALPH (laughs):
> You better not forget or I'll cut you out of my will. But
> listen, we'll have to go somewhere close. I'll only have
> a few minutes.

67.   CHARLOTTE AT PHONE

CHARLOTTE:
> We'll go to that Little Bohemian place. . . . Yes, I like
> the food there. . . . All right, then, at twelve.

She hangs up receiver. CAMERA TRUCKS BACK TO

68.   INT. LIVING ROOM OF SMALL APARTMENT
A modestly furnished room. There is a studio couch,
right, on which Florence has been sleeping. She straightens up, rubs her eyes, yawning, as Charlotte turns away
from phone.

FLORENCE (as Charlotte turns away from phone):
> Who was it? Penny ante?

CHARLOTTE:
> Yes, why?

FLORENCE:
> I wondered. Did he invite you to lunch, or did you
> invite him?[32]

CHARLOTTE:
> I wish you wouldn't be so sarcastic about Ralph. He's
> the sweetest kid I know.

Florence throws herself on bed, full-length, laughing.

CHARLOTTE:
> What are you laughing at?

FLORENCE:
> I just had a picture of you telling a landlady some day
> that you didn't have the rent, but Ralph is awful
> sweet.

CHARLOTTE:
> I don't see any big-moneyed boys running after you.

FLORENCE:
> I met one last night . . . all the money this side of Peoria.

CHARLOTTE:
> Did you? Where?

FLORENCE:
> In the can. (Charlotte starts.) The hoosegow! Mrs. Winton's little boy. The Pawk Avenue Wintons, you know . . . and plenty of do-re-mi. (Goes smoothly into melody of "Jail-house Blues." Singing.) He's in the jail-house now . . . [33]

LAP DISSOLVE TO:

69.   CLOSE SHOT AT HALL DOOR AT TOMBS OPENING[34]
Young Winton comes through and is led away by turnkey.

TURNKEY (addressing Ralph [sic]):
> Come on. Bring your stuff, you're goin' out.

70.   INT. OFFICE OF THE TOMBS
Two prosperous, middle-aged lawyers are seated near a desk talking to the official in charge. One of them is presenting a court order for Winton's release to the official.
The door opens and a turnkey leads young Winton into the room. Winton crosses quickly to the attorneys, both of whom rise, and, shaking hands with one, he laughs weakly.

WINTON:
> Mister, when I say I'm happier to see you than I ever was to see anybody in my life, you know that it comes from the heart. (Nodding to other man.) How are you, Mr. Gates?

96

SECOND ATTORNEY (shaking hands with Winton):
Splendid, my boy, splendid. What do you think you've been up to?

WINTON:
Not a thing.

FIRST ATTORNEY (laughs):
I hope your father accepts that statement.

WINTON:
Is Dad here?

SECOND ATTORNEY:
No. I talked to him long distance this morning.

WINTON:
Was he pretty sore?

FIRST ATTORNEY:
Well, he wasn't exactly overjoyed.

WINTON:
What did he say?

SECOND ATTORNEY:
He said to get you out of trouble and then hire someone to punch your head off. (All three laugh.)

FIRST ATTORNEY:
Have you had lunch?

WINTON:
No.

FIRST ATTORNEY:
Well, come on, we'll get something to eat.

They cross toward door.[35]

WINTON (to official behind desk):
Good morning.

OFFICIAL:
Hope to see you again soon.

97

WINTON:

I hope you don't.

They exit, laughing. The guard who brought Winton in looks after the departing men.

GUARD (as door closes behind them):

I'd give a year's pay to work on that puppy!³⁶

OFFICIAL:

But you don't shellac a guy when he can put up a hundred thousand dollar bail.

DISSOLVE TO:

71.   INT. OF TAXI CAB

Florence and Charlotte occupy the cab. Charlotte seems indignant but Florence is amused.

CHARLOTTE:

Well, I don't want to offend you, but, frankly, it's none of your business. I don't interfere in *your* affairs.

FLORENCE:

I don't have any affairs. What do you mean?

CHARLOTTE:

I don't think you could have a real affair. You couldn't care for anyone.

FLORENCE:

I've been in love so many times my heart is calloused . . . but I've never hit one with dough. This love-in-an-attic isn't my idea of a way to spend a pleasant afternoon.

CHARLOTTE:

I don't agree with you.

FLORENCE:

All right, you raise the kids—I'll raise the roof. I'd rather die with an athletic heart from shaking cocktails and bankers, than expire in a pan of dirty dish water.

CHARLOTTE:

You would.

FLORENCE:

He can look like a chimpanzee and act like an igorot but he must have dough—plenty of dough.

CHARLOTTE:

You think money is the only requisite. It happens that the poor people are happier.

FLORENCE:

Then marry Ralph . . . you'll be the happiest couple in the world.

DISSOLVE TO:

72. INT. MUSEUM A SHOT AT WINDOW

as Ralph, consulting his watch, approaches window and looks out. Through window we see a cab arriving. The two girls emerge from cab. Florence stops to pay driver.

As Ralph turns from window and starts for his hat and coat, CAMERA PULLS BACK TO A FULL SHOT. Ralph gets hat and coat and starts toward door. Igor, who has been near the front of museum, wheels out in front of Ralph.

IGOR:

And where do you think you are going, my good friend?

RALPH:

To lunch.

IGOR:

To lunch, you say. I am having coffee and sandwiches sent in. We are not leaving until we have everything ready for the opening.

RALPH:

But I have some friends waiting.

99

IGOR:
> That is unfortunate. They will have to wait.

RALPH:
> I will only be gone about half an hour.

IGOR:
> If you leave before the work is done, you will be gone for a much longer period . . . you will be gone for good.

RALPH:
> All right, I'll tell them. They're right here in front.

Ralph exits and CAMERA FOLLOWS him through the door.[37]

73.   EXT. MUSEUM ENTRANCE   CLOSE THREE SHOT
as Ralph enters to Charlotte and, taking both her hands, kisses her lightly on cheek. He speaks to Florence, who is standing beside Charlotte.

RALPH:
> Hello, Florence. How are you?

FLORENCE:
> Fine, thanks.

RALPH:
> Gee, honey-bunch, I'm sorry—I'm going to have to disappoint you.

FLORENCE:
> Don't worry—she'll get used to it.

She strolls up toward museum door, looking through it at interior.

CHARLOTTE:
> Disappoint me? Why, what do you mean, dear?

RALPH:
> Well, you see, the old chap is pretty anxious to open on schedule. All of his advertising announced the opening tonight.

As Ralph continues his explanation to Charlotte, CAMERA TRUCKS UP BEHIND Florence, and OVER HER SHOULDER THROUGH glass panel we see interior of museum with the various figures. Close to door we see the janitor carrying on his shoulder the Joan Gale figure which he places on a pedestal in foreground. He carries the figure in such a position that we see the back of it first, and as he places it on the pedestal he turns it around so that we see the face. CAMERA CONCENTRATES for several minutes on this figure.[38]

74.   CLOSE-UP   FLORENCE
Florence stares at it, puzzled. Then recognition dawns. Ralph enters PAST CAMERA and goes to door. He is about to hurry into museum, when Florence detains him by a hand on his arm. As she turns, we get the two in profile. Her expression is one of excitement.

FLORENCE:
> Listen, Genius, what're the chances for me to slip in and give this place the once over?

IGOR'S VOICE (heard through partly opened door):
> Ralph! Burton! Are you going to stay out there all day?

RALPH (drawing door to quietly and lowering his tone):
> I don't know . . . the old man's pretty peppery right now. Why don't you look in tonight?

FLORENCE:
> He might get some publicity out of it.

RALPH:
> No use. He's a crab, I tell you.

FLORENCE (looks through glass panel to Igor):
> Who? Old Santa Claus there? That's easy for anyone with my sex appeal. He's a pushover. Watch me stand that old dodo on his ear.

She pushes past Ralph and enters museum, followed by Ralph.

RALPH:
> Nix, Flo—he won't let you in and you'll only get me in Dutch.

FLORENCE:
> Horsefeathers![39]

75.   INT. MUSEUM
Igor sees a stranger entering with Ralph and wheels chair rapidly toward them, speaking as he goes.

IGOR:
> No visitors allowed! You people will have to get out!

FLORENCE:
> Aw, listen, Beaver, I'm from—

IGOR (interrupting—curtly):
> I don't care where you're from, young woman. I have said *no visitors!*

He suddenly looks up and sees Charlotte, who enters museum a bit hesitatingly. Igor stops speaking abruptly and sits, staring.

76.   CLOSE-UP   CHARLOTTE FROM IGOR'S ANGLE
We see Charlotte, smiling slightly. Then DOUBLE-EXPOSED over her figure comes the costume worn by Igor's Marie Antoinette in the London museum. This FADES IMMEDIATELY and we see Charlotte as she is, smiling at Igor.

77.   CLOSE-UP   IGOR
staring, fascinated. CAMERA DRAWS BACK to include the group again and Ralph notices something strange in Igor's manner.

RALPH:
> What's the matter, Mr. Igor?

IGOR (as though coming out of a trance):
Nothing—nothing at all, my boy. I should like to meet your friend.

Florence, taking advantage of the introduction, slips away, as CAMERA ANGLE WIDENS, and, to avoid suspicion, looks carefully at several figures during the following conversation, finally arriving before the Joan Gale figure, where she stops and studies the figure carefully.

RALPH:
Why, certainly, sir. My fiancée. Charlotte, may I present Mr. Igor.

CHARLOTTE:
Delighted, I'm sure. (Igor extends hand to her.)

IGOR:
If you will forgive this poor, crippled stump, my dear, I am very happy to know you.

CHARLOTTE:
Thank you.

IGOR (laughs whimsically):
Although you would be amused if I were to tell you that I knew you before you were born. Before this terrible thing happened to me . . . (His voice quavers.) . . . I made a very beautiful statue. Even if I had not met with this disaster, I could never have hoped to do anything finer, probably nothing quite so fine. And, my child, you are that figure come to life. I wonder, some time, would you pose for one of my sculptors who does very excellent work?

CHARLOTTE:
I'd love to, at any time.[40]

Florence, who seems to have satisfied herself as to the identity of the figure, turns abruptly and comes toward them.

FLORENCE:
> Well, I'm a woman who craves nourishment. Let's ankle out of here and find a beanery. Come on, Moon-struck. (Takes Charlotte by the arm.) Let's get going.

Sparrow, who has been hovering in the background, approaches the group and stands just behind Igor's chair. As Florence and Charlotte cross to door, Charlotte smiles back at Igor.

CHARLOTTE:
> We'll be coming to the opening.

IGOR:
> At any time. You will always be welcome.

FLORENCE (to Igor):
> So long, Pop, see you in jail.

Sparrow starts perceptibly.

RALPH:
> Until this evening.

The two girls exit.[41]

78.   EXT. IN FRONT OF MUSEUM
The two girls come from building and are starting toward corner when Florence, seeing a cab, signals to it. It swings in to curb.

FLORENCE:
> Listen, Kid, I'm going to leave you flat. I just thought of something and I've got to get to the office.

CHARLOTTE (running a few steps after her as Florence approaches cab):
> But what about lunch?

FLORENCE:
> I'll have it for supper. (Climbs into cab.) So long.

Cab swings away from curb. Charlotte stands looking after it, bewildered.

79.   INT. MUSEUM

Hugo and Ralph return to work. Sparrow stands beside Igor, who is addressing Ralph.

IGOR:

And you, young man, it is a matter to astonish one. You are engaged to that beautiful girl, who was just here. You have lived close to that beautiful creature, and yet you produce such caricatures as this. (Indicating Ralph's work.)

RALPH:

Charlotte is lovely, isn't she?

Igor, who seems to be in much better temper than we have seen him for some time, laughs.

IGOR:

Exquisite! But I am going to rechristen her for you, my friend. She is not to be Charlotte any more, she is Marie Antoinette.

Igor points to picture of himself and the figure of Marie Antoinette.

Sparrow, who has been standing near them, comes closer to Igor, as CAMERA MOVES UP TO CLOSE SHOT. A look of extreme cunning appears on his face.

SPARROW:

She is exactly like that statue?

Picture clearly shown on wall.

IGOR:

She is the soul of that statue.

SPARROW:

I wonder if I could have her pose for me.

CAMERA ANGLE WIDENS as Hugo laughs knowingly. Sparrow turns quickly and looks at him suspiciously.

SPARROW:
What are you laughing at?

IGOR:
He can't hear you.

Tapping himself on forehead, Igor indicates that Hugo is a little balmy.[42]

DISSOLVE TO:

80. EDITOR'S OFFICE
Florence enters.

FLORENCE:
Hello, Light-o'-my-life!

EDITOR (looking up):
Come in, Prussic Acid. What's on your mind?

FLORENCE:
I want to see the original pictures of Joan Gale.

EDITOR (into Dictaphone):
Hey, Mattie, dig into the morgue and send up all the art you have on Joan Gale.

A VOICE (answering through Dictaphone):
Right, Chief.

81. A LONG METAL FILING CABINET
A girl opens compartment marked *Ga.* Running through files, she extracts a number of photographs and walks out of scene.

82. EDITOR'S OFFICE

EDITOR (to Florence, who is sitting on edge of his desk):
Well, why so mysterious? Come on, spill it.

FLORENCE:

So you can give me an argument and tell me I'm wrong. Don't be sil, Kid.

The girl filing clerk enters and deposits pictures on desk.

EDITOR:

Thanks, Mattie.

MATTIE:

Yes, sir.

Florence has snatched the pictures from the desk and examines them carefully. Suddenly drops them on desk.

FLORENCE (getting to her feet):

I *am* right! I *know* I'm right!

EDITOR:

Well, no one would ever suspect it. You don't sound right.

Florence draws chair beside desk, drops into it and leans over, talking excitedly.

FLORENCE:

Listen, Jim—and if you wisecrack while I'm talking I'll crown you with the inkwell.

EDITOR:

All right, wise guy. Go ahead. Spill it.

FLORENCE:

Jim, there's a little hokey-pokey wax museum opening up down on 14th Street.

EDITOR:

Now don't that call for an extra!

FLORENCE:

I asked you to keep your trap shut!

EDITOR:

Well, you can't blame a guy for getting a little breathless with a scoop like that.

FLORENCE (rises indignantly):
All right, you poor baboon, you can guess the rest of it!

EDITOR:
No kiddin'. What's your idea?

FLORENCE:
Just this—I got a look at that dump a little while ago and if they haven't got a wax figure of Joan Gale in that line-up, then I'm crazy.

EDITOR:
We'll grant that.

FLORENCE:
What!

EDITOR (impatiently):
About the Gale girl, I mean. Where do we go from there? What of it?

FLORENCE:
Listen, Jo-jo. Does this mean anything to you? Joan Gale's body swiped from the morgue—Did you ever hear of such a thing as a death mask?

EDITOR:
I used to be married to one.

FLORENCE:
And it came to life and divorced you. I know all about that. Now my idea is this: Somebody swipes the girl's body, takes impression, makes a mold, produces wax figure . . . Bingo! . . . Peddles it to this old skate down there!

EDITOR:
Work that up into a comic strip and syndicate it.[43]

FLORENCE:
Let it go.

108

EDITOR:

> Come down to earth. Do you think they would dare do anything like that? Don't you think they'd know that figure would be recognized? Shake your head real hard—you'll be all right.

FLORENCE:

> All right, Master Mind. (Starts toward door.) But there's something cockeyed about that joint and I'm going to find out what it is.[44] (She gets to the door.)

EDITOR:

> Oh, by the way, another pet theory of yours just blew up.

FLORENCE:

> What do you mean?

EDITOR:

> That dear, innocent Judge Ramsey that you were so sure got bumped off for knowing too much has been located in South America.[45]

FLORENCE (with hand on knob):
> No kiddin'?

EDITOR:

> Almost certain.

FLORENCE (laughs—opens door):
> Almost! I'll still bet I'm right, and let you write your own ticket.

She exits.

FADE OUT

FADE IN

83.   EXT. STREET IN GREENWICH VILLAGE

Charlotte turns a corner and walks briskly TOWARD CAMERA, finally turning into an apartment about a quarter of the way down the block. As she disappears into the building, Sparrow appears around the corner and, walking past the building she entered, stops and lights a cigarette, inspecting the building immediately adjoining the apartment house. There is a large For Sale or Rent sign on the front of the building, giving the name and address of the agent handling the property. Sparrow goes to a basement door and tries it, finding it locked. He is investigating one of the windows when he sees that he is observed by a passer-by, and, taking a notebook from his pocket, apparently copies the name and address of the realty firm from the sign, and walks back in the direction from which he came, whistling.[46]

FADE OUT

FADE IN

84.   INT. LIVING ROOM   WINTON'S BACHELOR SUITE
Worth is standing near door. Winton, crossing to him, hands him a sum of money.

WINTON (as he counts money into Worth's hand):
    Well, that squares everything.

WORTH:
    Yep. Everything settled.

WINTON:
    Good. Well, I'll be seeing you.

WORTH (as he crosses to door):
    I'm glad they didn't hold you downtown.

WINTON:
    They didn't have a leg to stand on. There's no case against me. It's a clumsy thing to have happen, but nothing to worry about.

WORTH:
    Well, any time I can do anything for you—

WINTON:
    Thanks.

We hear the telephone ring and Winton crosses to answer it.

WORTH:
See you later. Good-by.

Worth exits.

WINTON:
So long. (Into phone.) Hello.

85.   CLOSE SHOT   TELEPHONE BOOTH

FLORENCE (into phone):
Hello. Is this Convict 87 thousand 412—and a
half?—Ho-ho, don't swoon.—This is the voice of the
New York Express broadcasting.

86.   A SHOT OF WINTON AT TELEPHONE

WINTON:
Oh, hello there. Say, I'm awfully glad you phoned. I
wanted to thank you for trying to cheer me up last
night.

87.   A SHOT OF FLORENCE IN PHONE BOOTH

FLORENCE:
How do you feel by now? . . . Yeh . . . Well, listen, if
you're grateful, you can prove it and maybe do yourself a good turn at the same time . . . Righto. Now at
about 8:30 tonight you be in your car at—
                                          DISSOLVE TO:

88.   EXT. VACANT BUILDING (WIND)   NIGHT
we saw Sparrow inspecting. Florence passes in front of
building and enters the apartment house adjoining. CAM-
ERA TRAVELS UP the front of the vacant building to the roof.

89.   EXT. ROOF OF VACANT BUILDING
We see a skylight forced open, the Monster clambers out
onto the roof and creeps stealthily to edge, peering into
lighted window of apartment house. CAMERA FOLLOWS
him. SHOOTING PAST him into room beyond, we see

Charlotte just putting the final touches to her toilette, preparing to put on dress. The Monster, gauging the distance carefully, springs across space separating buildings and clings to fire escape ladder like a huge monkey. He leans out from ladder and is about to raise window sash when the door of the room opens and Florence enters.

90.   INT. APARTMENT HOUSE ROOM
        Charlotte is dressing.

        FLORENCE:
            Come on, beautiful, leap into that loin cloth.

        CHARLOTTE:
            There's no hurry. It's early.

        FLORENCE (patting stomach):
            I can't convince the inner woman that we can wait. She's howling for a bit of ground beef before we drop in on Santa Claus and the other dummies. I've only had a cup of coffee since last night.

        CHARLOTTE:
            Why didn't you eat last night?

        FLORENCE:
            Ouch! Eat? You can do a solo if you don't step on it. I'm going to bow out on you.

        CHARLOTTE:
            What's the rush? There's no first act. They'll all be there and we don't have to appear at any particular time.

        FLORENCE:
            I'm hungry. I'll eat the first child I see. And I've an appointment with young Winton at 8:30.

        CHARLOTTE (seriously):
            You wouldn't get mixed up with that little rotter, would you?

FLORENCE:
> No? Give me a chance, baby. Money is music in my ears, and when his old man kicks off there'll be a million dollar tune.

CHARLOTTE (disgusted):
> If you're going to be indiscreet, I wish you'd be a little more discreet about it. Rich men, like Winton, love you and leave you.

FLORENCE:
> Yeah, but they leave you plenty.

91. EXT. ROOF OF VACANT BUILDING
The Monster has returned to the roof of vacant building. He shows a blind fury at the chance lost, and finally descends through skylight.

                                                  FADE OUT

FADE IN

92. EXT. MUSEUM
Standing beside the door is what appears to be a wax doorman in uniform. There are a number of curious people looking at the lobby display.

ONE OF THE VISITORS:
> Look at him now. Isn't that as real as life?

Now the figure suddenly moves his fingers, jerkily, as if he were a wax figure, then speaks.

SPIELER (walking up and down):
> Step right up, ladies and gentlemen. You can't afford to miss this exhibition that has thrilled the monarchs of the world. For the first time, America is privileged to see the collection pronounced by art lovers to be the finest in the world!

During this speech Florence and Charlotte enter the picture and start toward museum door.[47]

93.   INT. MUSEUM
We hear music coming from a modern victrola that changes records by itself. Igor, in wheelchair, is in front of statue of Sir Walter Raleigh, kneeling on a spreading velvet cloak on ground before the figure of Queen Elizabeth, who is smiling at him graciously.

IGOR:
The history of these figures, my friends, is more interesting, perhaps, when I tell you that the originals were destroyed twelve years ago in a fire in London, and restored only after years of arduous toil. To reproduce the figures destroyed I spent years training men to do the work that I can no longer do. Some of my workmen have trained for years before I would let them undertake a single figure of these groups that you have been looking at tonight.[48]

This has been a close shot of Igor and we assume that he has been addressing a rather large gathering, but as CAMERA SWINGS we see a pitifully small audience of not more than ten people.

94.   MAIN ENTRANCE OF MUSEUM
where Ralph is standing near door to receive visitors. CAMERA MOVES UP TO A

95.   CLOSE SHOT OF RALPH
As Charlotte and Florence enter, he takes a step forward to meet them.

RALPH:
Hello, hello. You're late. (Takes a step back from Charlotte and looks at her admiringly.) Gee, that's a pretty dress. Have I ever seen that before?

CHARLOTTE:
I think so.

FLORENCE:
Well, thank goodness, *that's* settled.

She walks directly to the figure she suspects, CAMERA TRUCKING after her.

96.   EXT. STREET IN FRONT OF MUSEUM
about four or five buildings removed from entrance. Winton, in roadster, pulls up to curb and looks up and down street expectantly. The barker is continuing his announcement through megaphone.

97.   INT. MUSEUM
Igor has ended his lecture, and Ralph is escorting a group of visitors to the door.

RALPH:
We hope you have enjoyed seeing these things to-night. I hope you will tell your friends for we believe we have something here of genuine public interest. (As the last of the visitors file through the door.) Good night. Thank you. Call again.[49]

98.   CLOSE SHOT OF FLORENCE
as she inspects the Joan Gale figure. We see that all doubt has been dispelled and that she is absolutely sure of her ground. Glancing about quickly, to be sure she is not observed, she stealthily sticks a pin into the arm of the figure as if convincing herself it is made of wax.

99.   SHOT OF IGOR
As the last of the visitors are leaving, Sparrow comes down behind him and, leaning over back of his chair, whispers something to him. Igor turns sharply.

IGOR (in intense, hushed tone):
Are you sure of that? Are you sure?

SPARROW:
I'd know him anywhere.

115

IGOR:

Don't lose sight of him. This is the most important thing in my life.

Sparrow sees Charlotte and Ralph approaching and signals Igor to silence. As Sparrow walks away, Ralph and Charlotte walk toward Igor smiling.

RALPH (in a rather encouraging tone):

I wouldn't feel too disappointed at the slimness of your audience tonight, Mr. Igor. The weather was against you, and the people are tired and getting over their celebration and preparing to go to work tomorrow.

IGOR:

Quite so. Quite so. (Extending hand to Charlotte who has been close beside Ralph.) And you, my little friend, my little Marie Antoinette. It is kind of you to be present.

CHARLOTTE:

But I think these things are beautiful.

IGOR:

They are. (To Ralph.) My boy, I think you are right. Everyone is tired out today and now that we have seen my doors open in a new country, I am beginning to realize that I am a little tired myself. You can call that fellow in from the front. I think we'll close for the night.

RALPH:

Yes, sir.

Ralph walks away toward the front door and CAMERA MOVES UP TO

100.   A CLOSE SHOT OF IGOR AND CHARLOTTE

IGOR:

I think I should have felt a little discouraged tonight but now everything seems quite as it should be. You know, to find just one person who appreciates my beautiful children here changes everything for me.[50] (He glances about to see that he is not observed, and continues.) You must come some time in the morning when there are no crowds about and I can give you more of my time.

Florence enters and breaks up the conversation.

FLORENCE:

Good evening, Mr. Igor. I've been admiring your works. Properly illuminated, they are more impressive than they were this morning.

IGOR:

Yes, for a time I despaired of ever achieving the same effects I had abroad. And then lighting came to my rescue.

FLORENCE:

I was particularly interested in that group over there.

She points and CAMERA SWINGS TO

101.   CLOSE SHOT OF CHARLOTTE CORDAY BENDING OVER FIGURE OF MARAT

IGOR'S VOICE:

Yes, that one is very fine. Its drama seems to interest people.

FLORENCE'S VOICE:

And this one, this single figure of Joan of Arc.

CAMERA SWINGS TO

102.   CLOSE SHOT OF THE JOAN GALE FIGURE

IGOR'S VOICE:
   That? Yes, that was the most recently completed. It
   only arrived this morning.

103.   OTHER CORNER OF SET
Ralph crosses in front of Sparrow.[51]

104.   SHOT OF IGOR, FLORENCE AND CHARLOTTE
showing length of museum and front entrance.

FLORENCE:
   You did this yourself?

IGOR:
   No, no, my friend. Never since these hands were
   burned have I created anything. I have only been able
   to direct the work of others.

FLORENCE:
   But who did it?

Sparrow, who has been standing in background during
the preceding dialogue, listening nervously, now shows
extreme uneasiness as Igor replies.

IGOR (pointing):
   Professor Darcey. He has been my hands for years.

105.   CLOSE-UP   SPARROW
He shifts nervously and laughs self-consciously.

106.   INT. CLOAKROOM   REAR OF MUSEUM
The deaf and dumb man on scene as Ralph enters. Ralph,
slipping into overcoat, scarf, etc., slaps him on the back.

RALPH (yelling):
   Good night!

The mute chuckles inanely as Ralph makes his exit. After
Ralph is gone, Hugo takes a black, loose ulster—a couple

118

of sizes too large—and hat from the hook, his clothes resembling those worn by the Monster. Slipping into them, he exits from cloakroom and disappears through a rear door.

107.   INT. MUSEUM
The janitor comes up the steps from Igor's private work-room. He looks to the entrance to the street and we see

108.   IGOR
just bidding good night to Florence, Charlotte and Ralph.

109.   THE JANITOR
glancing about and feeling that he is unobserved, crosses quickly to the statue of Joan Gale and raises his hand as though to caress it, when Sparrow appears from behind another figure, grinning evilly.

SPARROW:
   Good night.

The janitor starts guiltily and slinks quickly out through rear door.

110.   EXT. STREET IN FRONT OF MUSEUM
Sparrow comes from museum and turns to the right out of picture, but calls to the others who are still standing in doorway.

SPARROW:
   Good night.

Florence shows agitated concern in looking after the re-treating figure of Sparrow.

111.   EXT. STREET NEAR MUSEUM
Winton, seated in roadster. He catches sight of Florence and sounds the auto horn. She sees him and waves.

112.   EXT. ENTRANCE OF MUSEUM

FLORENCE (to Ralph and Charlotte):
    You people will have to struggle along without me.
    There's my heavy date. No fouling in the clinches!

She runs toward car.

113.   EXT. STREET   WINTON'S CAR
Florence getting into roadster.

FLORENCE (breathlessly):
    Hurry up! Tail that little runt down the street!

In extreme background we see Sparrow turning a corner,
then we see the car follow quickly and turn the corner after
him.

114.   EXT. STREET NEAR MUSEUM   CHARLOTTE AND RALPH
CAMERA FOLLOWS them as they walk down the street.

RALPH:
    I wish you'd cut her out and get a place by yourself.
    (Looking after Florence.)

CHARLOTTE:
    But why? She's the best friend I've got.

RALPH:
    She isn't anybody's friend, and I don't like you living
    with her. She's a bad influence.

CHARLOTTE:
    Nonsense. She's one of the nicest girls I know.

RALPH:
    What's nice about her? . . . a hard-boiled little gold
    digger.

CHARLOTTE (heatedly):
    I won't let you say that!

RALPH:

Well, I *do* say it.

CHARLOTTE:

She thinks it's funny to talk the way she does, but—

RALPH (interrupting):

Don't kid yourself—she means it.

CHARLOTTE:

Are we going to have the same quarrel over again?

RALPH:

I'm not quarreling, only . . . [52]

DISSOLVE TO:

115.   EXT. STREET THAT SPARROW IS TRAVERSING
The car, with Winton and Florence, loafing a block in the rear.

116.   CLOSE SHOT   WINTON'S CAR

FLORENCE:

Don't ask any questions right now. I think we're on the trail of hot news.

DISSOLVE TO:

117.   EXT. STREET   CHARLOTTE AND RALPH
Their argument has grown rather heated.

CHARLOTTE:

Yes, certainly I would. And I'd be terribly disappointed if you were stupid enough to object to it.

RALPH:

You wouldn't have said that before you met her.

CHARLOTTE:

I'd call it stupid at any time.

RALPH:

Well, that's just how stupid I am. When you go riding, it will be with me. And if it's with someone else, you can make it a permanent arrangement.

CHARLOTTE (stops and draws her arm away from him):
So that's the way it is?

RALPH:
That's the way I feel about it.

CHARLOTTE:
I'm glad you told me. Good night, Mr. Burton.

Turning, she walks rapidly away. Ralph stands, looking after her.[53]

DISSOLVE TO:

118. EXT. WORTH'S HOME
where we saw the mysterious box delivered. Sparrow walks into picture and rings bell beside door on street level. After a short pause, the door is opened and he disappears through it. The car carrying Winton and Florence passes the house and, going to the next corner, stops.

WINTON:
Don't you think this would be as good a time as any to break the news to me? What's it all about?

FLORENCE:
Well, as one of the interested parties, I suppose I might as well tell you the glad tidings. I think the fellow we've been following had something to do with the robbery at the morgue.

Winton shows nervousness and distaste.

WINTON:
Now look here. It's not up to us to do our own detective work. I've had enough trouble over this matter. I don't want anything more to do with it.

FLORENCE:
Not even if it gives you a clean bill of health?

WINTON:
Not even then. The police are the proper people to

conduct this affair. Now if you've got any suspicions I'll drive you to the nearest police station.

FLORENCE:

What! And let every rag in town grab a red-hot story? Not so you could notice it! Now, look, I want you to drive me around the corner and wait for me.

WINTON:

I told you I didn't want to mix in it.

FLORENCE (jumping from car):

All right, brother. Then you can go to some nice warm place, and I don't mean California.

She starts back toward Worth's house. Winton overtakes her.

WINTON:

Please. I'm sorry. I'll see it through. What do you want me to do?

FLORENCE:

I told you what to do. Drive around the corner out of sight of the house. I want to get a closer look at the place.

He starts back toward car.

119.   INT. WORTH'S OFFICE IN HOUSE
Worth is seated at the desk and Sparrow is standing in front of him. Worth is speaking.

WORTH:

You're yellow to the core—just yellow.[54]

SPARROW (whimpering):

No, I'm not. But I've had the uncanniest feelin' that someone's been watchin' me.

WORTH (laughs):

Nobody's watching you. You're yellow and your

nerves are gone. And let me tell you, I'll do nothing to help your nerves until it's delivered, and you might as well get that through your head.

SPARROW:
All right, then, I'll phone.

He reaches for the phone on Worth's desk. Worth snatches it away from him.

WORTH:
Not over this phone, you fool! Get outside to make the call.

SPARROW:
Okay, Boss.

Sparrow turns, walks TOWARD CAMERA.

120. EXT. FRONT OF WORTH'S HOUSE
Florence comes in and pauses and, glancing quickly up and down the street, runs down steps to basement door, which she tries cautiously. Finding it locked, she tries to peer through window, and finally tries lower sash, which opens. She climbs through window to basement.

121. EXT. CORNER OF STREET
where Winton is waiting. The street door of house opens and Sparrow appears, starting away in opposite direction from corner where Winton waits.

122. INT. BASEMENT ROOM IN WORTH'S HOUSE
Florence is feeling her way about. She passes in front of mirror, sees her own reflection, jumps back, startled, trips and sits down heavily on a pine box that might contain a coffin. She gasps and springs to her feet, terrified.[55]

123. EXT. CORNER OF STREET
Two plain-clothes men approach Winton and address him.

FIRST DETECTIVE:
Well, buddy, what's the stall?

WINTON:
I'm waiting for someone.

FIRST DETECTIVE:
Yeah, for who?

WINTON:
I don't think it concerns you.

SECOND DETECTIVE:
Come on, Winton. Cut out the bluffing. We've been watching you ever since you left The Tombs and you've done some pretty suspicious things. Now what are you doing here?

WINTON:
What have I done that's suspicious?

FIRST DETECTIVE:
For one thing, you had a visitor at your apartment today, not exactly the kind of a person I'd expect you to entertain . . . a person who lives in this block.

124. INT. BASEMENT IN WORTH'S HOUSE
Florence is raising up from inspection of box when she sees the reflection of the Monster in mirror and drops down behind the box. The figure of the Monster glides into the room, stands as though listening for a moment and then disappears in shadows. We hear someone ascending a flight of rickety stairs.

125. EXT. CORNER OF STREET   WINTON AND TWO DETECTIVES

WINTON (pointing down the street excitedly):
I've got to follow that fellow, I tell you. I've reason to believe he knows what became of Joan Gale's body. You've no right to stop me.

FIRST DETECTIVE:
  Hang onto him, Paul. I'll get the other bird.

He starts off in the direction Winton had pointed. In extreme background we see Sparrow occasionally as he passes under an arc lamp. The detective follows him, walking rapidly. As detective passes Worth's house,[56]

CUT TO:

126. CLOSE SHOT OF BASEMENT WINDOW
Florence clambering through and hurrying up the stairs. She is chattering with fright. She gets to the top of the stairs, stands and sways, almost falls.

127. EXT. CORNER OF STREET   LONG SHOT
Florence running toward Winton and detective. CAMERA FOLLOWS her to a

128. CLOSE SHOT OF THE THREE
Florence grabs Winton by the shoulders and speaks hysterically.

FLORENCE:
  I found it! I found the body!

DETECTIVE:
  What! What are you talking about?

FLORENCE:
  The body of Joan Gale!

DETECTIVE (getting a look at Florence):
  Hello, Express. What's the idea, trying to outsmart the police?

FLORENCE (seriously):
  I'm not kidding. Joan Gale's body is packed in the box in the basement, and I saw the most horrible thing down there.

DETECTIVE:
  Are you giving me this straight?

FLORENCE:
> Don't take my word for it. Get down there yourself
> and give a look.

The officer blows police whistle.

129.   CLOSE SHOT OF SPARROW
just coming under street lamp. We hear a police whistle
back of him. He turns, looks back, terrified, and darts
away at a quick run.

130.   CLOSE SHOT OF OFFICER
back of him, also breaking into a run. We hear the sound
of night stick being struck against the sidewalk and police
whistles from different directions and at various dis-
tances.

131.   EXT. STREET IN FRONT OF WORTH'S HOUSE
The detective, Winton and Florence are approaching.
Several uniformed policemen are running toward them
from both intersecting streets. There is an *ad lib* confused
babble of voices as a number of curious people approach
the house from several directions.

FIRST DETECTIVE (to Winton):
> Get this skirt out of here! We don't need hysterics.
> This thing has to be handled smoothly.

Winton tries to take Florence away. She tears loose.

FLORENCE:
> Listen, copper, get a load of this. While you're chin-
> ning yourself on a bar rail, I run down this story . . .
> *my* story. Consider yourself my assistant.

DETECTIVE:
> What do you think I am?

FLORENCE (shrugging):
> Whatever you are, you're the only one of it.

DETECTIVE:
It happens that I'm the law.

FLORENCE (producing police card):
How quaint. But I can go any place you can. (Shows her credentials.)[57]

132.   INT. OFFICE IN WORTH'S HOUSE
We see Worth cross the room and go through a door into an adjoining room. Then we hear a doorbell ring rapidly. The Monster appears through the door Worth just made an exit through, comes to the center of the room and stands listening. Evidently they become tired of ringing, with no response, for we hear them start to batter in the door. The Monster turns and vanishes quickly the way he came. We hear the door shattered and, after a moment's pause, an officer appears stealthily, with drawn revolver, around the hall door of the room.

OFFICER:
Nobody here, Chief.

FIRST DETECTIVE (peering through door):
Well, take it easy. Let's get some light on here. (Officer flashes flashlight in search of switch.)

FIRST DETECTIVE (calls into hallway):
A couple of you fellows get upstairs!

VOICES (off scene):
Yes, sir.

We hear them ascending the stairs. Officer crosses and gingerly opens door of room that the Monster disappeared through, flashes light about and enters.

133.   INT. ROOM ADJOINING WORTH'S OFFICE
There is only the one entrance door, and the window of the room, when the officer examines it with flashlight, appears to be flat against the brick wall of the adjoining house. The room is empty.

134. INT. WORTH'S OFFICE
The detective, evidently finding switch, has thrown on lights. He is talking to Florence and Winton.

DETECTIVE:
Can you give me a description of the person you saw?

FLORENCE:
Not a very good one, I guess. He wasn't like anything human. He hobbled and swayed like a monkey, and the face, from the glimpse I got of it in the light from the street, was like an African war mask.

DETECTIVE:
You mean he was colored?[58]

FLORENCE:
I don't know what he was, but he made Frankenstein look like a lily! [59]

The officer comes in from the adjoining room.

OFFICER:
Well, there's nothing on this floor.

We hear the men descending stairs from floor above. The detective steps to the door.

DETECTIVE (calling):
Did you find anything up there?

A VOICE (off scene—as of someone approaching):
No—not even any furniture up there—a lot of old papers and junk.

The two uniformed policemen enter from hall.

DETECTIVE:
Is there any rear entrance to this place?

POLICEMAN:
I couldn't find any.

129

DETECTIVE:
Well, let's give the basement a look.

135. INT. HALL IN WORTH'S HOUSE
The officers and detective, with Florence and Winton, approach basement door and cautiously start to descend steps to basement.

136. INT. BASEMENT OF WORTH'S HOUSE
Two uniformed men enter and flash lights everywhere. One of them tries door to rear room. It opens. They turn back and shout.[60]

POLICEMAN:
No one here.

Lights come on as though switch were thrown on other side of partition. Florence, Winton and two detectives enter, followed by the two uniformed policemen.

FLORENCE (points to the box):
There she is! You'll find Joan Gale in that box.

WINTON (sinks back against wall and gasps):
No—No—I—I—I don't want to see it. (Starts toward door.)

DETECTIVE:
Wait a minute! You stay right where you are. (To one of the policemen as he sees a small hatchet on a table.) Get that hatchet and open this up.

One officer gets the hatchet and the others drag the box a little nearer the center of the room and they start to pry off the lid. As they pull one nail, it comes out with a mournful shriek. Florence almost falls over a smaller box in her effort to get away.

FLORENCE:
Oh, what wouldn't I give for a slug of gin!

With a terrific ripping sound, they finally succeed in removing the lid. Everybody crowds forward to peer at what they believe to be a corpse, as CAMERA COMES TO A

137.   CLOSE-UP OF THE BOX
its contents revealed to be row on row of bottles of Scotch whiskey. An officer's hand comes in and lifts out a bottle. CAMERA DRAWS BACK TO

138.   MED. SHOT OF THE ROOM

FLORENCE (sinking back onto box, extending hands and wiggling fingers):
    Oh, gimme, gimme!

There is a general shout of laughter and the basement door opens and the second detective enters, driving Sparrow ahead of him.

SPARROW (blubbering):
    I ain't done nothin'—you ain't got no right to arrest me! What's the charge against me?

The detective slaps his face.

DETECTIVE:
    Now, who owns this layout? Come on, spill it.

SPARROW:
    I don't know. I was never here before tonight.

DETECTIVE (slaps him again):
    You don't know, oh . . . You don't know anything about it.

SPARROW:
    No. All I know is there was a fellow named Worth—

WINTON:
    Worth!

SPARROW:
    Yes, sir, that was his name.

WINTON:
> That's my bootlegger's name! Was he a heavyset fellow, with a stubby moustache?

SPARROW:
> Yes, sir, that's the bird.

WINTON (laughs):
> I hope he delivered the stuff I paid him for this afternoon. (Then, remembering—to detective.) I *told* you it was a bootlegger you saw at my place.

DETECTIVE (to one of the uniformed policemen):
> Here, take this fellow in.

One of the policemen leads Sparrow out roughly.

SPARROW (as he goes):
> I ain't done nothin'. I wouldn't even deliver some stuff for him.

Florence starts piling bottles of whiskey on her arm like an armload of cordwood.

DETECTIVE:
> Hey, what do you think you're doing? Put that stuff back!

FLORENCE:
> Nothing doing. This is my percentage. You birds are going to get yours. And anyhow, *I* found this dump.

She exits, followed by Winton. There is a general laugh.[61]

> DISSOLVE TO:

139. LARGE WHITE BULB AT ENTRANCE OF POLICE STATION SHOWING PRECINCT NUMERALS
CAMERA PULLS BACK showing Winton seated in car near entrance. A policeman is taking Sparrow up the steps. CAMERA FOLLOWS them in.

140.   INT. POLICE SERGEANT'S OFFICE
Sergeant looks up as policeman and Sparrow enter.

SERGEANT:
    Junky, eh.

POLICEMAN:
    Yeh—peddling. (To Sparrow.) Put up your hands!

Sparrow holds up his hands. The policeman searches him, laying articles from his pocket on desk before sergeant. Among the articles is a very handsome watch. The sergeant looks at it.

SERGEANT:
    A classy turnip. Must have dipped it.

Lays it on desk with a pile of other things.

141.   INT. POLICE CAPTAIN'S OFFICE
Captain is seated at desk. He is laughing heartily at Florence.

FLORENCE:
    Imagine my embarrassment. The razzing I'm going
    to get is nobody's business. I tail a corpse and stumble on a box full of spirits and not a dead one in the
    layout.[62]

CAPTAIN:
    They tell me your managing editor is poison.

FLORENCE:
    Poison! It takes a sturdy person to look at him!

They are both laughing as the door opens and the policeman enters, leading Sparrow.

POLICEMAN:
    You want to talk to this fellow, Captain?

CAPTAIN (glancing at Sparrow contemptuously):
    No, that's all right, Denny. He's a junky. He'll talk in a
    little while. Just lock him up.

133

POLICEMAN:
Yes, sir. (To Sparrow.) Come on.

He leads Sparrow out.

DISSOLVE TO:

142.   INT. HORROR CHAMBER
We have not seen, up to this point, anything that would give us a clue as to the location of this room, which we now see for the first time. It is a stone room, with apparently but one opening through a trap in the ceiling, which is approached by a spiral stairway. There are several huge vats of some steaming liquid, a few pieces of dilapidated furniture and an embalming table in the center of the room.
   The Monster descends steps, carrying the body of a man, wrapped in burlap. He places it on table.[63]

DISSOLVE TO:

143.   INT. POLICE STATION   CAPTAIN'S OFFICE

FLORENCE (rising):
Well, the season's best catch is out there waiting in his Rolls-Royce. I guess I'll breeze.

CAPTAIN:
Well, you ought to get a good laugh story out of it, anyhow.

The door opens. A man in uniform, but hatless, enters quickly and, coming to desk, lays the watch taken from Sparrow before the captain.

OFFICER:
What do you think this is?

CAPTAIN (grinning):
Looks like a watch.

OFFICER:
Yeh, but do you know *whose* watch?

134

FLORENCE:
> Let's break down and confess—we don't know any-
> thing about it.

Officer opens the back of the watch and holds it so that she
can read the inscription on inner case.

OFFICER:
> Judge Ramsey's! That's all!

CAPTAIN (reaching out for it quickly):
> What!

FLORENCE:
> You're not kiddin'?

CAPTAIN:
> Where did this come from?

OFFICER:
> Just took it off that junky.

CAPTAIN:
> Great! Get him down here.

FLORENCE:
> Now you're talking.

DISSOLVE TO:

144. EXT. STREET IN FRONT OF POLICE STATION
Winton seated in car. Florence runs down steps and
climbs into car.

FLORENCE:
> The office! There's not much traffic—you can step
> on it!

WINTON (as car pulls away from curb):
> You like taking chances, don't you!

145. INT. CAR RACING UP BROADWAY   CLOSE SHOT

FLORENCE:
> Why?

WINTON:
You go in for dangerous things.[64]

FLORENCE:
Darned if I don't! (Reaches over quickly with left hand and pulls steering wheel.)

146.   REVERSE ANGLE   THROUGH WINDSHIELD
Showing narrowly averted collision.

FLORENCE'S VOICE:
Slow down to ninety. I said the office, not the cemetery.

147.   INT. OF CAR   CLOSE SHOT

WINTON:
No, really. I mean what I'm saying. I never believed there were women like you in the world. You're game and decent.

They narrowly miss striking another car.

FLORENCE:
—and so determined to live that I'm going to get out and take a taxi if you don't watch where you're going.

WINTON:
I suppose this is going to sound absurd. I've only known you twenty-four hours, but I'm in love with you.

FLORENCE:
It doesn't usually take that long, but I'll forgive you—you were in a tough spot when I met you.

WINTON:
No, really—I'm crazy about you.

FLORENCE:
Oh, is that what caused it?

WINTON:
> You don't believe me. You think I'm just talking. Will you marry me?

FLORENCE:
> How much money have you got?

WINTON:
> Heaven knows. A lot.

FLORENCE:
> Well, that being the case, I'll take it up with the board of directors. Hey, listen, aviator, here we are!

The car swings into the reporter's entrance of the Express Building.

FLORENCE:
> Hold everything. I'll be right back.

148. INT. EDITOR'S OFFICE
The editor is just finishing phone conversation.

EDITOR:
> All right. Give that a four-point head. No, that's all it's worth . . . All right, you can play it up later if . . .

Door opens and Florence comes in, breathless, extends hand.

FLORENCE:
> Mit me, kid. I've got a classic.

EDITOR (looking at her with a melancholy expression):
> You here again like an evil spirit to mar my happiness?

FLORENCE:
> This one's a story, but I'm not going to tell you what it is. Every time I tell you anything it goes haywire.

EDITOR (laughs):

What do you mean—haywire? You start out after murderers and come back with three-for-a-dime bootleggers. You start to solve murder mysteries and break up crap games. You're grand! *I'm for you!* Stupendous!

FLORENCE (steps toward his desk belligerently):

Say, you're always razzing everthing I do, but this is one time I'm in.

EDITOR:

Go on, little girl, take your troubles somewhere else. I don't feel like talking to you.

FLORENCE:

Was there any art on Judge Ramsey?

EDITOR (laughs):

What goofy idea have you got now? Don't tell me you suspect Judge Ramsey of stealing the body.

FLORENCE (goes to door):

I'm going to make you eat dirt, you soap bubble! I'm going to make you beg for somebody to help you let go![65]

FADE OUT

FADE IN

149. INT. POLICE STATION   CAPTAIN'S OFFICE[66]

Sparrow is seated in the center of the room, quivering for want of the drug. A number of detectives, in shirt-sleeves, evidently worn and tired themselves, are circling about the room.

FIRST DETECTIVE:

So you found the watch in a taxi cab three months ago. Is that right?

SPARROW:

Yes, sir. I got in the cab and it was layin' there on the floor.

FIRST DETECTIVE:
Where were you going when you got in that cab?

SPARROW:
I don't remember. No so very far—

FIRST DETECTIVE:
Don't remember what day that was, do you?

SPARROW:
No, sir. About three months ago.

SECOND DETECTIVE:
Remember what kind of a cab it was?

SPARROW:
No, sir. Just a cab.

FIRST DETECTIVE:
You didn't happen to be going to Worth's place, did you?

SPARROW:
No, sir, I'm sure it wasn't there.

FIRST DETECTIVE:
You used to go to Worth's place a whole lot. What makes you sure it wasn't there?

SPARROW:
Well, maybe it was. I don't remember. (Sparrow slips from chair to knees, sobbing.) You got to do something for me, I can't stand it any longer—I can't!

150.   CLOSE SHOT   TWO DETECTIVES STANDING NEAR WINDOW

ONE OF THE DETECTIVES:
He's beginning to break now—he'll talk pretty soon.

OTHER DETECTIVE:
I don't know about that—he's been begging all night.

Looks out of window and we see that it is almost daylight.

OTHER DETECTIVE:
>Nearly half past eight. I never saw a junky hold out like this before.

FADE OUT

FADE IN

151.   EXT. MUSEUM   THE NEXT MORNING

The people passing are of the type who would be hurrying to report for some office or clerical job around nine o'clock. Charlotte walks into picture, glances up and down street as though looking for someone, then glances at watch and goes to museum door, peering through panel. She tries the door and finds it open and enters.

152.   INT. WAX MUSEUM   LONG SHOT

Nobody is in scene. Charlotte enters, looks about.[67]

CHARLOTTE (calling):
>Ralph! Are you here?

There is no answer and she starts down the length of the museum, occasionally calling "Ralph." As she passes a niche in the wall that contains a half figure of Dante on the platform, the CAMERA MOVES TO CLOSE-UP of that figure. The artificial lids are raised and we see the eyes of a living person peering through and watching her progress. Over this we hear her calling "Ralph" again, but the call is growing fainter. The lids drop back into place.

CUT TO:

153.   CLOSE SHOT   NEAR PORTIERES

Charlotte is near portieres which conceal door to workshop at rear. She draws curtains aside and steps into workshop.

CUT TO:

154.   INT. WORKROOM AT REAR

Hugo is at work. Charlotte has advanced several steps into the room before she becomes aware of his presence. She stops, startled.

140

CHARLOTTE:

I beg your pardon—Is Ralph here?

There is no response as Hugo does not hear her. She advances a step farther, when he turns and grins at her.

CHARLOTTE:

I'm looking for Ralph.

Hugo, still grinning, takes a step toward her and makes the hideous sound identified with deaf-mutes. She starts to back away from him, terrified.[68]

Backing toward portieres, followed by Hugo, she suddenly turns and darts through the curtains. Her momentum carries her almost to Igor, who is approaching in wheelchair. She extends both her hands to him delightedly. He starts to respond, then, catching sight of his crippled claws, drops them into his lap.

CHARLOTTE:

Oh! Mr. Igor!—I'm so glad you're here—I don't know why I should be, but I was a little bit afraid.

IGOR:

Oh! So, my little friend, you have honored me by accepting my invitation of last night.

CHARLOTTE:

No—I—wanted to speak to Ralph. We had a silly argument last night and I said something unkind.

IGOR (laughs in a tender, fatherly way):

Oh, you children, you happy children. You've quarreled and now you're going to be friends again. And that is as it should be. Never let any stupid misunderstandings come between you.

CHARLOTTE:

But it was really my fault.

IGOR (laughs):

And he will probably demand the life of anyone who

agrees with you. Let him think it was his fault . . . He should be along very shortly . . . But be very stern before you forgive him, especially if it *was* your fault . . . *While you're waiting for your friend, would you like to see some new figures I have downstairs? [69]

CHARLOTTE:
I'd love to.

CAMERA FOLLOWS them as Igor wheels to top of stairs leading to studio and workshop below. He takes crutches and struggles painfully to his feet.

CHARLOTTE:
Oh, please, Mr. Igor, I'm terribly ashamed. I shouldn't have put you to so much trouble.

IGOR (chuckles gently):
It is no trouble at all, my child. This is the strange, vicarious pleasure that remains for me—to see others enjoy the beauty I used to create. (He attempts to descend first step, then says, good-naturedly.) My footing is not too secure.

Charlotte rushes to his assistance.

CHARLOTTE:
Oh, let me help you, please.

Charlotte helps him descend stairs.*

155.   SHOT PHOTOGRAPHED THROUGH OPEN DOOR OF BASEMENT
WORKSHOP TOWARD STAIRS
We see Charlotte and Igor finish descending steps.

IGOR:
Thank you—thank you, my dear.

Charlotte precedes Igor into room and stands glancing about. Igor enters, closes the door quickly and locks it. [70]

156.   INT. WORKROOM
Igor instantly drops his crutches and sweeps Charlotte into his arms, lifting her clear of the floor.

IGOR:
    Marie Antoinette.

Charlotte screams and struggles.

CHARLOTTE:
    Let me go! Let me go!

IGOR:
    We have found immortality, you and I. You must not be afraid.

CHARLOTTE (screams):
    Ralph! Ralph!

She tears at Igor's face and rips away the mask and beard, which bring with them the skillfully designed wig that is attached to them, revealing the horribly mutilated face of the Monster. Charlotte screams and faints. Igor deposits her tenderly on a couch and kneels beside her.[71]

157.   INT. WORKROOM   CLOSE SHOT
Igor, kneeling beside the girl, speaks.

IGOR:
    Poor, frightened child. The only common objective of all living things is death . . . and she is afraid.[72]

158.   EXT. FRONT ENTRANCE OF MUSEUM
Janitor is sweeping walk. Ralph comes into picture, glances into museum and, assuming that he is the first to arrive, takes a last puff on a cigarette before entering. He throws it away and starts to enter when we hear Florence's voice off scene.

FLORENCE:
    Hey—Ralph!

He looks up and we see that he recognizes someone approaching, as Winton's car whirls up to the curb and Florence jumps out, followed by Winton.[73]

RALPH:
What are you people doing out in the middle of the night?

FLORENCE (crossing to him):
I'm after news, as usual. I wonder if it would be all right for me to slip in and look around your factory?

RALPH:
I guess so. But wouldn't it be better for you to wait until the old man's here?

159. CLOSE SHOT RALPH AND FLORENCE

FLORENCE:
Well, I'll tell you a secret. I kinda like the old gent and I'm trying to build a special Sunday Magazine story out of him. It might help him a whole lot. But that's a side issue—something I do on my own time.

RALPH (boyishly):
Gee, that's great. After the bad opening that night the old boy was pretty blue. This will pep him up. Have you told him about it?

FLORENCE:
No. I wanted to do it without saying anything. I think he's worth it.

160. EXT. MUSEUM A SHOT OF WINTON'S CAR
A policeman walks up to car and calls over to group.

POLICEMAN:
Whose car is this?

WINTON:
Mine.

POLICEMAN:
Well—You can't park there. You'll have to take it down the street.

WINTON (going to car and climbing back to wheel):
Okay, brother. (Shouts to Florence.) Flo, I've got to find a place to park. I'll be right back.[74]

CAMERA ANGLE WIDENS taking in Ralph and Florence at museum door.

FLORENCE (waves to Winton—calls):
Don't deceive me or I'll come back and haunt you.

Winton's car moves away. Ralph unlocks the door, and he and Florence enter the museum. Ralph throws away cigarette. Janitor picks it up and stands leaning on broom, puffing it.

161. INT. MUSEUM
Florence takes from her bag a photograph of Judge Ramsey.
INSERT: CLOSE-UP OF PHOTOGRAPH
showing bust picture of man whose features are strikingly like those of Voltaire, although he has a moustache, wears glasses and is dressed in modern clothes.

CAMERA TRUCKS AFTER her as she goes from one figure to another, finally stopping in front of the figure of Voltaire. This she studies, in profile, full-face three-quarter view, etc., and finds by comparison that the two are identical.
    (We CUT back and forth several times from the photograph to the statue.)

FLORENCE (studying the photo and wax figure; she is nervously biting her fingernails):
Ralph, come here a minute, will you?

RALPH (crossing to her and notices her biting nails):
Better cut that out. (Points to figure of Venus de Milo.) That's what happens to girls who bite their nails. (Florence ignores the remark.) What's wrong?

145

Hugo passes them at this moment. Florence watches Hugo suspiciously as if she did not want him to know what she is referring to. She waits until he has passed into the cloakroom.

FLORENCE:
Look at this photograph, will you? (Handing Ralph photograph.)[75]

162.   INT. POLICE STATION   CAPTAIN'S OFFICE
Sparrow suddenly springs to his feet, screaming.

SPARROW:
All right—I'll talk! I'll tell you what I know! (He is a madman.) Ramsey was murdered because he looked like Voltaire! (He laughs wildly.) Because he looked like Voltaire! You want to know what became of him! He's a statue—a silly wax statue! (Laughs.)

CAPTAIN:
You killed him! (Catches Sparrow roughly, wheels him around, slaps his face.) Come on with the rest of it. You killed him!

SPARROW:
No—I didn't. It was Igor at the waxworks.

CAPTAIN (slapping him again):
But you were in on it—you worked for him.

SPARROW:
No—the only thing I did for him was to keep track of the man named Worth that runs the place where you arrested me tonight.

CAPTAIN:
You lie!

SPARROW:
It's Igor at the Wax Museum! You'll find your judge embalmed in wax! He's a statue of Voltaire, with all

146

the other corpses! The whole place is a morgue—do you hear?—a morgue! (Laughs.)

163.   INT. HORROR CHAMBER
Charlotte is crouched, terrified, in a corner, while Igor, now a raving maniac, tries to calm her.

IGOR:
My child, why are you crouched there? So pitifully afraid. Immortality has been the dream, the inspiration of our kind, and I am going to give you the only guarantee of immortality you have ever had.

Charlotte shrinks further into the corner.

CHARLOTTE (gasping):
Please, oh, please, I haven't done anything to hurt you.

IGOR (in bewildered, plaintive tone):
And I have no desire to hurt you. You will always be beautiful. Think, my child, in a thousand years you will be as lovely as you are now.[76]

164.   INT. MUSEUM
Ralph is holding the photograph, and he and Florence stand looking at the figure. We see that the features of the two are identical. Then we hear a muffled scream. Florence and Ralph look at each other inquiringly and stand waiting for the scream to be repeated.

165.   INT. HORROR CHAMBER
The Monster is pleading with Charlotte.

IGOR:
My child, my child, if you will just listen to me, then you will not be afraid. Don't you understand, dear, that I love you? Don't you know that at times when I have wanted to die—I could not die because I had not saved you. And now you are here, to be given, a

thing of delight, to all the world. I am trying to grant you immortality.[77]

Charlotte is just a terrified, half-hypnotized, crumpled mass.

CHARLOTTE (almost whispering):
You fiend! You fiend!

Igor backs away from her, gesturing with his arms as if to ward off a blow.

IGOR:
Oh, my Marie Antoinette, you must not say that to me. There *was* a fiend, of that you may be sure. There was a fiend—(suddenly extends hands toward her)—and this is what that monstrous person did to me.

166.   CLOSE SHOT OF CHARLOTTE
as she drops her head on her knees, sobbing.

167.   EXT. POLICE STATION
Officers pour out and climb into two cars. They commandeer a couple of taxis and all race down the street, with sirens screaming.

168.   INT. HORROR CHAMBER   FULL SHOT
Igor standing over Charlotte pityingly, wringing his hands. Then he whirls toward curtained cabinet in rear.

IGOR (screaming):
You! . . . You did this! (To Charlotte, as he crosses toward cabinet.) These terrible broken hands—this terrible living dead man—for twelve years, twelve awful years, has hunted for the fiend, the fiend who brought us here tonight! But the account is closed. (He sweeps aside curtain covering cabinet.) He is here!

148

In the cabinet, full length, erect, is the wax-embalmed figure of Worth, which falls forward stiffly, landing with a thud. Charlotte gives a piercing, terrified scream.

169. INT. MUSEUM
Florence and Ralph hear scream repeated and rush to stairs. CAMERA FOLLOWS them as they run to stairs and start down. They find door locked. Ralph throws his full weight against the door several times. When the door shatters he stumbles into room.

170. INT. WORKSHOP
They look around, startled. It is apparently untenanted. As they stand looking at each other in bewilderment, the scream is repeated. Ralph gestures, "Wait a minute," then, with emphasis:

RALPH:
It *did* come from under our feet!

Searching about, he finds a trap door, which he opens and looks down, and sees:

171. SHOT FROM RALPH'S ANGLE
We see Charlotte on operating table. The Monster is stirring a huge vat of boiling wax. Hearing the trap door open, he looks up, sees Ralph and screams his rage. Ralph passes CAMERA and starts downstairs toward him.

172. INT. WORKSHOP   CLOSE SHOT OF FLORENCE
standing at trap, looking down, horrified. She whirls and dashes, screaming, upstairs toward the museum.

173. INT. HORROR CHAMBER
Ralph and the Monster having a furious struggle, the Monster attempting to force the boy backward into one of the vats of boiling wax.

174.   INT. MUSEUM
Florence appears at head of stairs from below, just as
Winton enters door. She runs to him.

FLORENCE (screaming):
    Come on! Quick! Help!

As they descend the stairs.

WINTON:
    What is it? What happened?

FLORENCE:
    Don't ask any questions. Come on!

175.   INT. HORROR CHAMBER
The Monster succeeds in striking Ralph over the head
with some heavy object. As Ralph sinks, stunned, to the
floor, the Monster dashes up the steps.

176.   SHOT FROM HORROR CHAMBER CAMERA TIPPED UP
SHARPLY
showing trap at head of stairs. When the Monster has
negotiated three-quarters of the ascent, we see Winton
appear in the trap door above, blocking his escape. Now
we hear the screaming of the sirens of approaching police
cars. Seeing his passage barred, the Monster, no longer
coherent, stands jabbering like an infuriated ape at the
man above him.

177.   INT. WORKSHOP
Winton at edge of trap, looking down, horrified.

FLORENCE:
    Do something! Can't you? Do something!

Winton draws back. Florence turns, runs back toward
museum, screaming. We hear the tramping of feet on the
floor above and then see the feet and legs of first officer
descending stairs.

178. SHOT UPWARD FROM HORROR CHAMBER
As Winton draws from trap, the Monster starts to advance. A policeman in uniform appears above him, with drawn revolver.

POLICEMAN:
Get 'em up! Don't move!

He commences a cautious descent of the stairs. CAMERA PULLS BACK TO

179. FULL SHOT
We see Ralph, who has recovered, gather Charlotte in his arms and whirl her so that his body would shield her from a possible stray bullet. The Monster, who is backing, still defiant, before the policeman, misses his footing and, with an agonizing scream, whirls downward into a vat of boiling wax.[78]

180. EXT. STREET IN FRONT OF MUSEUM
A great crowd is collecting. The police are holding them back. They lead the janitor and Hugo from the building.

CAPTAIN OF DETECTIVES:
I don't think these mugs mean anything, but take them around and get a statement from them.

An officer leads them away. Florence runs through crowd with Winton.

181. EXT. STREET   WINTON'S CAR
as Florence and Winton scramble in.

FLORENCE:
Come on, pal, get me uptown! (Breathlessly.) Don't stop for lights—don't stop for—

182. EXT. STREET IN FRONT OF MUSEUM
Ralph is leading Charlotte, still hysterical, through door.[79]
DISSOLVE TO:

183.   INT. COMPOSING ROOM NEW YORK EXPRESS

Before the room is clearly discernible, we hear the clatter of typewriters. A scene of feverish activity. Copy boys are dashing back and forth. The place is seething with excitement. Florence, seated at machine nearest CAMERA, is typing frantically. She evidently just completes the last line of story, jerks sheet from machine and hands it to a copy boy.

FLORENCE:
Take it away, Hennessy. (Springs to her feet.)

She is bedraggled, hair hanging in her eyes, evidently exhausted. She reels toward the editor's room. Several desk workers spring up and surround her, traveling a part of the distance with her. They are thumping her playfully on the back and talking.

FIRST MAN:
My hat's off to you, kid. What a scoop!

SECOND MAN:
This story makes history.

THIRD MAN:
Congratulations, Flo. You've got the other papers bleeding.

FLORENCE (laughing):
Now I'm going to scramble this egg.

Points toward door marked Managing Editor.

184.   INT. EDITOR'S OFFICE

He looks up as Florence enters room. She is gloating.

FLORENCE:
Well, Poison Ivy, how about it? Was that a story?

He looks up sourly.

EDITOR:
Lousy! You had a million dollars worth of luck.[80]

She looks at him indignantly.

FLORENCE:

Listen, stupid, could I do *anything* that would possibly meet with your approval?[81]

EDITOR:

Yes, you could. Cut out this rotten business and act like a lady. Marry me.[82]

She hears the honking of an automobile in the street below and walks to the window, looks down for a moment.

185.   SHOT FROM FLORENCE'S ANGLE   WINTON IN CAR

in front of the Express Building, honking impatiently.

186.   INT. EDITOR'S OFFICE

Florence turns back from window, grins at editor.

FLORENCE:

Marry you?

EDITOR:

That's what I said.

FLORENCE:

I'm going to get even with you, you dirty stiff! I'll do it!

He rises and catches her in his arms.[83] As they embrace, we hear the raucous "honk-honk" of the car in the street below.

FADE OUT

THE END

Annotation to the Screenplay

1 In the film, 1921.
2 Lionel Atwill, as Igor, is first mentioned in the script of September 1, 1932.
3 The September 1 script changed the owner's name from Wells to Worth, probably because the name of the villain in *Doctor X* is also Wells.
4 The policeman is dropped in the film.
5 Dialogue in this scene is not in the film.
6 Scene 8 does not appear in the film.
7 No references to Sidney Carton, Sir Walter Raleigh, and Joan of Arc are made at this point in the film.
8 In the film, the following dialogue is substituted for that between the asterisks in the text:
GOLATILY: But tell me, where did you begin to model in wax?
IGOR: In my native country, at first as a hobby.
RASMUSSEN: He had a great reputation as a sculptor.
IGOR: Oh, you are very kind, sir. However, I was commissioned to come to England, and at the completion of my work I turned my mind more seriously to these, because it seemed to satisfy me more. I felt I could reproduce the warmth and flesh and blood of life far more better in wax than in cold stone.
9 Dialogue between asterisks is not in the film.
10 In the film, the action described in this paragraph is covered by fifty-one shots.
11 The script of August 9, 1932, contains a brief scene here showing Igor in a hospital bed, heavily bandaged. "Dr." Rasmussen tells him: "We will not have to amputate your hands, my poor friend, but I am afraid you will never create again." Igor's eyes fill with tears.
12 In the film, the clock announces 1933.
13 In the August 22 script, we are to see a big close-up of the face.
14 This script is the first version in which the embalmed body rises, a touch borrowed from *Doctor X*.
15 In the film, scene 31 is restructured so that we start with the attendants; we don't see the Monster until they leave, and all his action comes later.

16 Glenda Farrell is first mentioned in the September 1 script.

17 Scene 33 does not appear in the film.

18 Frank McHugh is first mentioned in the September 1 script.

19 Scene 36 does not appear in the film. The film goes directly to scenes 41–46, although all dialogue is cut until "I thought I told you to stay out of here" in scene 45. Then back to scenes 37–40, followed by 47–.

20 Sparrow's identification as a "cocaine fiend" is first made explicit in he September 1 script.

21 The first mentioned of laudanum poisoning occurs in the August 22 script.

22 Dialogue between asterisks is not in the film.

23 This line is not in the film.

24 This speech is not in the film.

25 Igor's line is not in the film, nor is the action with the whiskey bottle.

26 All the preceding action in scene 59 was cut from the film.

27 In the film, "One of the Athenian girls for the bacchanal."

28 In earlier treatments, Igor asks, "Are you God?" and then "Are you *the Creator*?" Censorship required the change.

29 Igor first calls Sparrow "Professor Darcey" in the August 22 script.

30 This line and Igor's preceding one are not in the film.

31 In the film, we see a long shot of Charlotte doing exercises in her room as the phone rings. Fay Wray is first mentioned in the September 1 script.

32 In the film, the dialogue from scene 71 has been inserted here.

33 Much of the dialogue in scenes 65–68 and 71 has been rearranged. In the film, Florence sings "The Prisoner's Song" ("If he had the wings of an angel . . . ").

34 Scene 69 opens instead with a shot of books being pushed aside.

35 The remaining dialogue in scene 70 is not in the film.

36 In the September 1 script, this reads "that bloke."

37 Scene 72 does not appear in the film.

38 Instead of this action, we see Florence walk around the museum, looking at several exhibits.

39 Scene 74 does not appear in the film.

40 At this point in the film, there is a new sequence showing Florence climbing up on the Joan of Arc display. She finds a morgue label (?) in a box at its foot and pockets the label, but a hand immediately picks the label out of her pocket.

41 In the film, Ralph leaves with the girls and the scene ends with the following dialogue:

SPARROW: I assume I shall have the privilege of having her pose for me?

IGOR: That was my plan.

SPARROW: Thank you.

42 Scene 79 does not appear in the film.

43 This exchange indicates how self-censorship cleaned up Florence's dialogue. The August 22 script reads:

FLORENCE: You—(we do not hear the rest—only see the lip movement as she says) s-- of a b----.

EDITOR: What's that?

FLORENCE: When you get home, throw your mother a bone.

In the September 1 script, this is changed to "Florence mumbles something inaudible," and then the line about the bone. Here it has disappeared altogether, although similar exchanges do survive in the film.

44 As she says this line in the film, she discovers that the label she found in the museum is missing from her pocket.

45 Sir Cecil was dropped after the August 9 treatment, and Judge Ramsey took his place in the August 22 script.

46 Scene 83 does not appear in the film.

47 Scenes 88–91 do not appear in the film. In place of scene 92, the film has a tracking shot moving across the marquee and a shot of people entering the museum.

48 This scene is expanded in the film as Igor discusses some of the groups in his exhibit: Sir Walter Raleigh and Queen Elizabeth, Marat and Corday, Maximilian, Napoleon, and others.

49 Scene 97 does not appear in the film.

50 In the film, Igor adds here, "You are very beautiful," and Charlotte answers, "Thank you." Then a cut to Florence, examining the Joan of Arc figure and scraping wax from its foot, followed by a shot of Winton pulling up in his car outside the museum.

51 Scene 103 does not appear in the film.

52 Scene 114 does not appear in the film.

53 Scene 117 does not appear in the film.

54 In the August 22 script, he scowls, ". . . and you call yourself British."

55 In the film, there is a more elaborate search sequence, which includes some comedy. Scene 122 runs directly into scene 124, emphasizing the appearance of the Monster more strongly. Scene 123 follows scene 124.

56 Scene 125 does not appear in the film.

57 In the film, scene 131 contains no dialogue.
58 In the August 22 script, the detective asks, "You mean he was a nigger?"
59 This version of the script is the first to carry the reference to Frankenstein.
60 At this point in the film, there is a comedy bit in which a gun suspiciously appears from behind the door but turns out to belong to two other policemen.
61 In the film, this scene ends as Florence sees a large packing crate sliding aside like a secret doorway. She screams, drops the bottles, and runs out.
62 This speech is not in the film.
63 In the film, scene 142 follows scene 143. Scenes 141 and 143 run together with slight dialogue changes.
64 The August 22 script has the following dialogue here:
    WINTON: You seem to go in for Nitsche [*sic*].
    FLORENCE: Nitsche [*sic*]—not often.
    WINTON: You remember he said: Live dangerously and you will never be bored.
    FLORENCE: Darned if he didn't.
65 In the film, she follows this with: "You may be the world to your mother, but you're a . . . " (conclusion lost in editor's horse laugh).
66 This scene is preceded by a shot of a clock face reading 8:20 and the voice-over dialogue: "Let's get them some coffee. They've been in there with that junkie all night."
67 In the film, we see Hugo follow her and lock the door.
68 In earlier treatments, Charlotte simply walks in and immediately meets Igor.
69 In the film, the following dialogue is substituted for that between the asterisks:
    IGOR: Now I understand why he was so gloomy this morning.
    CHARLOTTE: Then he's here?
    IGOR: Yes, down in the workroom. I'll call him for you.
    CHARLOTTE: No, please don't bother. I think it would be better if I surprise him.
    IGOR: As you wish, my child. Just go straight ahead.
    CHARLOTTE: All right, thanks.
    There is a lengthy sequence showing Charlotte wandering through menacing corridors, calling for Ralph, and finally arriving down in the "workroom."
70 Scene 155 does not appear in the film.

71   Instead of this action, the film uses the following scene:
     IGOR (wheels himself in through a doorway): What's the matter, my
         child, are you afraid?
     CHARLOTTE: But I thought you said Ralph was here?
     IGOR: I came to tell you that I was mistaken. I sent Otto to find him.
         Well, I hope this little glimpse behind the scenes will interest
         you. This is the birthplace of all my creations. Let me show you
         . . . (He starts to move.)
     CHARLOTTE: Oh, I don't want to put you to the trouble, Mr. Igor.
     IGOR: Oh, it's no trouble at all, my child. This is the strange vicarious
         pleasure that remains for me, to see others enjoy the beauty I
         used to create. (He starts to rise.) My footing is none too secure.
     CHARLOTTE: Oh please, let me help you.
     IGOR: You will help me, my dear. You will help me give back to the
         world my masterpiece. (Standing.) My Marie Antoinette!
     Charlotte screams. Florence and Winton arrive outside in his car; a
     policeman tells him to move it elsewhere.
72   Scene 157 does not appear in the film.
73   As described in note 71, Winton has already driven off to park the car.
74   This action takes place earlier (see note 71).
75   The dialogue is cut from this scene, since Florence looks at the photo
     without Ralph.
76   Now Charlotte strikes him, breaks the mask, and screams.
77   Igor's speech here is cut from the film and replaced with:
     CHARLOTTE: Your face—was wax! You fiend!
     IGOR: My Marie Antoinette, you must not say that to me. . . .
     CHARLOTTE: You fiend!
78   Scenes 175–79 are substantially different in the film. After striking
     Ralph, Igor pulls the table with Charlotte over to one side and says (in
     apparently dubbed-over dialogue): "Don't be afraid, my dear. In a
     few minutes the container will have filled with wax. And when it
     overflows, your beauty will be preserved forever." He turns a series
     of dials and gets the equipment into operation, closing an automatic
     trap door that locks out Florence and Winton. He prepares to inject
     Charlotte with an oversized hypodermic. The police arrive, break
     through the trap door with a packing crate and invade the labora-
     tory. Igor fights off four of them as the bubbling wax begins to
     threaten Charlotte. Finally the police shoot him and he falls from a
     catwalk into the molten wax. Ralph awakes just in time to save
     Charlotte from the wax machine.
79   Scenes 180–82 do not appear in the film.

80 In the August 11 script, the editor also cracks, "You're covered with horseshoes," but this line was later deleted.
81 In the August 11 script, she says, "Listen, Bum," but this is crossed out in pencil and "stupid" substituted. The censorship requirements of the British market called for this change.
82 In all previous treatments the editor says, "Act like a woman . . . "
83 In the August 22 script, the editor has the last word: "Come here, tramp."

Production Credits

Director	Michael Curtiz
Screenplay by	Don Mullaly and Carl Erickson
From the story by	Charles S. Belden
Edited by	George Amy
Art Director	Anton Grot
Assistant Director	Frank Shaw
Photographed in two-color Technicolor process by	Ray Rennahan
Camera Operator	Dick Towers
Stills Cameraman	Scotty Welbourne
Gowns by	Orry-Kelly
Make-up by	Perc Westmore
Wax figures by	L. E. Otis, assisted by H. Clay Campbell
Vitaphone Orchestra conducted by	Leo F. Forbstein

Running time: The film lasts 78 minutes, according to the press book and the copyright catalog. But the press book gives the length of the film as 7,184 feet, which, at sound speed, would run for 79 minutes and 49 seconds. Released: February 1933.

Cast

Ivan Igor	Lionel Atwill
Charlotte Duncan	Fay Wray
Florence	Glenda Farrell
Jim (the editor)	Frank McHugh
Ralph Burton	Allen Vincent
George Winton	Gavin Gordon
Joe Worth	Edwin Maxwell
Dr. Rasmussen	Holmes Herbert
Golatily	Claude King
Sparrow	Arthur Edmund Carewe
Detective	Thomas Jackson
Police captain	DeWitt Jennings
Hugo (called Otto in the film)	Matthew Betz
Joan Gale	Monica Bannister
Janitor (called Otto in the script)	Bull Anderson
Plain-clothes man	Pat O'Malley

Inventory

The following materials from the Warner library of the Wisconsin Center for Film and Theater Research were used by Koszarski in preparing *Mystery of the Wax Museum* for the Wisconsin/Warner Bros. Screenplay Series:

Story Outline, "The Wax Works," by Charles S. Belden, January 4, 1932, 12 pages.

Treatment, "Wax Works," by Don Mullaly, July 27, 1932, 32 pages.

Treatment, "The Wax Works," by Carl Erickson, July 30, 1932, 13 pages.

Treatment, "The Wax Works," by Mullaly and Erickson, August 9, 1932, 48 pages.

Treatment, "The Wax Works," by Mullaly and Erickson, August 11, 1932, 48 pages.

Screenplay, "The Wax Works," by Mullaly and Erickson, August 22, 1932, 103 pages.

Temporary, "Wax Museum," by Mullaly and Erickson, September 1, 1932, 99 pages.

Final, "Wax Museum," by Mullaly and Erickson, September 22, 1932, with changed pages to September 30, 1932, 108 pages.

DESIGNED BY GARY GORE
COMPOSED BY GRAPHIC COMPOSITION, INC.
ATHENS, GEORGIA
MANUFACTURED BY THE NORTH CENTRAL PUBLISHING CO.
ST. PAUL, MINNESOTA
TEXT AND DISPLAY LINES ARE SET IN PALATINO

ⓌⒿ

Library of Congress Cataloging in Publication Data
Main entry under title:
Mystery of the wax museum.
(Wisconsin/Warner Bros. screenplay series)
1. Mystery of the wax museum (Motion picture)
I. Koszarski, Richard.   II. Title.
PN1997.M97   812'.5'2   78-53296
ISBN 0-299-07670-9
ISBN 0-299-07674-1 pbk.

The Wisconsin/Warner Bros. Screenplay Series, a product of the Warner Brothers Film Library, will enable film scholars, students, researchers, and aficionados to gain insights into individual American films in ways never before possible.

The Warner library was acquired in 1957 by the United Artists Corporation, which in turn donated it to the Wisconsin Center for Film and Theater Research in 1969. The massive library, housed in the State Historical Society of Wisconsin, contains eight hundred sound feature films, fifteen hundred short subjects, and nineteen thousand still negatives, as well as the legal files, press books, and screenplays of virtually every Warner film produced from 1930 until 1950. This rich treasure trove has made the University of Wisconsin one of the major centers for film research, attracting scholars from around the world. This series of published screenplays represents a creative use of the Warner library, both a boon to scholars and a tribute to United Artists.

Most published film scripts are literal transcriptions of finished films. The Wisconsin/Warner screenplays are primary source documents—the final shooting versions including revisions made during production. As such, they will explicate the art of screenwriting as film transcriptions cannot. They will help the user to understand the arts of directing and acting, as well as the other arts involved in the film-making process, in comparing these screenplays with the final films. (Films of the Warner library are available at modest rates from the United Artists nontheatrical rental library, United Artists/16 mm.)

From the eight hundred feature films in the library, the general editor and the editorial committee of the series have chosen those that have received critical recognition for their excellence of directing, screenwriting, and acting, films that are distinctive examples of their genre, those that have particular historical relevance, and some that are adaptations of well-known novels and plays. The researcher, instructor, or student can, in the judicious selection of individual volumes for close examination, gain a heightened appreciation and broad understanding of the American film and its historical role during this critical period.